All About Poetry

Cheshire & Merseyside

Edited by Charlie Fletcher

This book belongs to

First published in Great Britain in 2010 by

Young**Writers**

Remus House
Coltsfoot Drive
Peterborough
PE2 9JX
Telephone: 01733 890066
Website: www.youngwriters.co.uk

All Rights Reserved
Book Design by Spencer Hart
© Copyright Contributors 2010
SB ISBN 978-0-85739-019-6

Foreword

At Young Writers our defining aim is to promote an enjoyment of reading and writing amongst children and young adults. By giving aspiring poets the opportunity to see their work in print, their love of the written word as well as confidence in their own abilities has the chance to blossom.

Our latest competition *Poetry Express* was designed to introduce primary school children to the wonders of creative expression. They were given free reign to write on any theme and in any style, thus encouraging them to use and explore a variety of different poetic forms.

We are proud to present the resulting collection of regional anthologies which are an excellent showcase of young writing talent. With such a diverse range of entries received, the selection process was difficult yet very rewarding.

From comical rhymes to poignant verses, there is plenty to entertain and inspire within these pages. We hope you agree that this collection bursting with imagination is one to treasure.

Contents

Bishop Martin CE School, Woolton
Louise Vickers (10) 1
Caurie-Jade Morgan (10) 2
Erin Ellis (9) 2
Stephen Lennox (9) 3
Emma Norris (10) 4
Marley Davies (10) 5
Catrina Kenward (9) 6

Broadstone Hall Primary School, Stockport
Sara Ahmed (9) 6
Jade Leishman (10) 7
Hannah Redfern (8) 7

Capenhurst CE Primary School, Capenhurst
Ellie Doyle (10) 8

Castleway Primary School, Moreton
Abisaliny Arunprakash (10) 8
Joel Barrow (9) 9
Jade Brereton-Weir (9) 9
Kirsty Beaty (9) 10
Chloe Murphy (9) 10
Megan Innes (9) 11
Sophie Maughan (10) 11
Bethany Price (9) 12

English Martyrs RC Primary School, Litherland
Jessica Handley (9) 12

Gainsborough Junior School, Crewe
Berfim Katranbayiri 12
Paige Leek & Shuhro Mahmud 13
Isobelle Cooper 14
Andraya Ball (10) 14
Bethan Lewsley 15
Tayniah Benson 15

Halsnead Community Primary School, Whiston
Libby Graham (8) 15
Chloe Liderth (10) 17
Cerys McStein-Roberts (10) 17
Alicia Harrison (9) 18
Danielle Pickering (9) 18
Marley Dwyer (10) 19
Megan Lee (8) 19
Katie Thompson (9) 19
Zachary Edmondson (9) 20
Chloë J Nelson (10) 20
Sophie Richardson (7) 20
Heather Beesley (7) 21
Amy Tegg (9) 21
Chloe Nicole Carmichael (9) 21
Amy Cinnamond (9) 22
Kieran Leather (9) 22
Daniel Bates (9) 22
Laylah Scott (9) 22

Ladymount RC School, Wirral
Ewan Herd (7) 23

Newton Bank Preparatory School, Newton-le-Willows
Millie Bolton (9) 24
Charlotte Crook (10) 24
Tayler Brown (10) 25
Nikhil Mediratta (8) 25
Zarah Mughal (9) 26
Iona Molyneaux Townshend (8) 26
Darren Bettany (7) 27
Finnley Shufflebotham (8) 27
Charlie Morris (10) 28
Rosie Robinson (9) 28

Our Lady of Pity RC Primary School, Wirral
Olivia Davies (9) 29
Molly Nelson 29
Melissa Heller (8) 30

Isobella Cromby-While (9)	30
Andrew Walsh (8)	31
Anya Brown (8)	31
Rachel Holland (9)	31
Mathew Lightfoot (7)	32

Our Lady Star of the Sea Primary School, Seaforth
Ellen Cook (8)	32
Ryan Thurlbeck (9)	33
Caitlin Rose Eileen Mullin (8)	33
Emily Moore (8)	34
Conor Donnelly (9)	34
Jack Moore (8)	35
Ryan Quinn (9)	35
Mia Shaw (8)	35
Dylan Gibney (8)	36

Our Lady's Catholic Primary School, Warrington
Holly Kitchingman (11)	36
Ruby-Rose McGann (10)	37
Tyra Hamblett (10)	38
Lydia Smith (10)	39
Ben Tavlin (11)	40
Sharna Boyle	41
Daniel Marsh (10)	42
Sophie Logan (11)	43
Brittany Leah (10)	43
Rebecca Savage (10)	44
Andrew Smith (11)	44

Penketh Community Primary School, Penketh
Marian Eilidh Unwin (8)	45
Molly Weir (8)	45
Abbie Taylor (8)	46
Faye McGrath (9)	46
Gemma Clarke (8)	47
Matthew Wright (9)	47
Gabrielle Andrus (9)	48
Lee Robert Wilson (9)	48
Courtney Swindell (8) & Molly Wooldridge (9)	49
Tyler Westwood (9)	49
Hannah Carver (8)	50
Jordan Edge (8)	50
Jack Taylor (8)	51
Harry Bromwell (8)	51

Rosie Burgess (9)	51
Alexander Zachariah Winstanley-Venables (9)	52
Ellie Roberts (8)	52

Plantation Primary School, Halewood
Lauryn Huxley (11)	53
James Horn (11)	53
James Mullings (11)	54
Ben Harper (10)	54
Rachael Kofoed (10)	55
Lewis Green (11)	55
Millicent Mae Lawlor (9)	56
Holly Mulhearn (9)	56
James Higham (10)	57
Eleanor Stock (9)	57
Elliot Fewtrell (10)	58
Caitlin Lloyd (11)	58
Alexandra Greenwood (10)	59
Adam Smith (11)	59
Ryan McCrae (10)	60
Sophie Baugh (10)	60
Jack Gargan (11)	61
Aaron Ellis (10)	61
Megan Humphreys (11)	62
Owen Mulhearn (10)	62
Lydia Stratulis (10)	63
Abbie McHugh (11)	63
Arron Muirhead (10)	64
Jennifer Edwards (10)	64
Karla Jordan (9)	65
Nathan Williams (10)	65
Lauryn Goulding (10)	66
James Critchley (8)	66
Jamie Andrews (9)	67
Bethany Smith (10)	67
Lauren Owen (10)	68
George Panther (10)	68

Prestbury CE Primary School, Prestbury
Harry Aldrich & Lucy Wilkinson	68
Emma Crook (9), Lauren Gardner (9) & Sam Lawson (10)	69
Grace Goddard (9)	69
Alexander Moss (10)	70
Emily How (9)	70

Freya Massie (9) & Molly Ellison 71
Sophia Lyon & Euan Davies................. 71
Hattie Bennett (9) 72
Nomi Fischer (9).................................... 72
Molly Williams (10) 73
Verity Partington (9) 73
Amelia Naden (9) 74
Emily Green (9) 74
Katie Pain & Mairi Florence.................. 75
Noah Seaborn (9).................................. 75
Sophie Hiscott (9) 76
Pippa Wyer (9)...................................... 76
Cameron McFarlane (9) 77
Eleanor Bradley (9)............................... 77
Annalise Arkinstall (9) 78
Kirsty Turpin (9).................................... 78
Oliver Luckman & Harry Simpson (9) .. 79
Marcus Jack Keenan,
Alexander Dinnis & Anna Palk (9) 79
Dulcie Whadcock (9)
& Trudi Pennington (10)........................ 80
Lucy Ridgeway & Roisin Tooher (9) 80

Prospect Vale Primary School, Cheadle
Sophie Parker (10)................................ 80
Jasmine Furness (8)............................. 81
Emily Carson (7) 81
Mohammed Ali (10)............................... 82
Hannah Evans (10)................................ 82
Charlotte Brunt (11)............................... 83
Sophie Clayton (7)................................ 83
Ellen Corser (11) 84
Maisie O'Neill (7) 84
Aram Shayan (9) 85
Lara Saxe (11)...................................... 85
Rachel Carson (10) 86
Molly Martin (8)..................................... 86
Maleehah Awan (9) 87
William Corser (8)................................. 87
James Cottrell (10)................................ 88
Sonam Rathour (9)............................... 88
Molly O'Rourke (9) 89
Samuel Jack Longman (9) 89
Haider Sattar (9)................................... 90
Fizah Mahmood (9)............................... 90
Ben Cottrell (10) 91
Holly Saxe (8) 91

Megan Clayton (10).............................. 92
Olivia Cash (10).................................... 92
Daniel Dabell (10)................................. 93
Maria Chaudry-Hassan (7) 93
Daniel James King (10)........................ 94
Edward Wordingham (10).................... 94
Nicola Diane Hall (10) 95
Orla-Kate O'Neill (9) 95
Zahra Choudhry (9) 96
Sanah Saghir (7) 96
Aaliyah Forbes (10) 97
Safah Choudhry (7).............................. 97
Hassan Rasul (9).................................. 98
Sarah Sweeney (8) 98
Kamran Chaudhry (10)......................... 99
Kate Gibbons (11)................................ 99
Alex Robertson (10)............................ 100
Ben Mills (8).. 100
Sonia Rathour (9) 101
Thomas Pattinson (10) 101
Adam Pervez-Jan(11)......................... 102
Sam Crompton Whittle (8).................. 102
Rebecca Hall (11) 103
Kimya Arkian (8) 103
Maddy Prescott (8)............................. 104
Zara Ashraf (11) 104
Mollie Hayes-Johnson (11) 105
Bradley Clegg (8) 105
Sajeel Choudhry (10) 106
Robert Broughton-Smith (10).............. 106
Erin Naughton (8)................................ 107
Saba Amjid (8) 107
Rebecca Mulligan (9) 108
Jack Stelfox (7)................................... 108
Kobe Nelson (7) 109
Muazzam Naru (11)............................ 109
Aliza Mian (10).................................... 109

Rose Hill Primary School, Marple
Eve-Marie Connolly (10)..................... 110
Ella Dina Vanstone (10)...................... 111
Lara Garrett (10)................................. 111
Amy Smith (10)................................... 112
Sarah Tetlow (11)............................... 112
Harry Turner (10)................................ 112
Jemma Cliff (10) 113
Jack Rowbottom (10)......................... 113
Cameron Stone (11)........................... 113

St Andrew the Apostle School, Halewood
Olivia Norris (8) 114
Caitlin Eyres (7) 114

St Gregory's Catholic Primary School, Bollington
Emily Rafferty (10) 115
Ellie Collins 115
Michael Revell (9) 116
Anna Bishop (8) 116
Ellie Richards (7) 117
Izzy Hughes (10) 117
Isabel Quigley (10) 118
Alex Needham (11) 118

St Mary's Catholic Primary School, Crewe
Jodie Rowlands 118
Jessica Prophett 119
Chloe Webster (11) 119
Blake Bratherton (9) 120
Tara Moir 120
Lesley Anne Fox 121
Trina Casanova (10) 121
Isaac Orr (9) 122
Lauren Clarke 122
Summer Shannan (10) 123
Abby Lockett 123
Leah Blake 124
Jordan Owen (9) 124
Caitlin Bayley 125
Issy Pountain 125
Megan Brown (10) 126
Aiqing Lu (11) 126
William Ward 127
Gabby Williams 127
Daniel Cooper (9) 128
Ellie Bolland 128
Emily Gresty (11) 128
Saffron Baldwin 129

St Michael's Primary School, Widnes
Emma Corby (11) 129
Callum Grimes (11) 130
Bethany Nolan (9) 130
Molly Fillingham (10) 131
Elliott Jenkins (11) 131

Caitlin Parker (10) 132
Shannon Mercer (9) 132
Nathan Jones (7) 133
Curtis-Lee Campbell (11) 133
Louise Follon (9) 134
Jack Clemson (7) 134
Rhea Butterworth (8) 134
Daniel Carroll (8) 135
Frankie Carson (7) 135
Dillon Barrow (8) 135
Ellie Naughton (11) 136

Sunnymede School, Birkdale
Luke Jamieson (9) 136
Nathan Chinn (9) 137
Tosin Oyebola (10) 137
Charles Carney (10) 138
Joshua Quinlan (9) 138
Isabella Knowler (9) 139
Skye-Bleu Trevalyan (9) 139
Katie Howard (9) 140
Sam Harris (9) 140
Emma Pitman (9) 141

Winwick CE Primary School, Winwick
Emily Wallbank (11) 141
Eleanor Smith (11) 142
Sandra Habeeb (11) 142
Elliott Brooks (10) 143
Emily Noble (11) 143
Matthew Gardner (10) 144
Hannah Peake (11) 144
Brooke Lee (10) 144
Matthew Hansley (11) 145
Cody Griffiths (11) 145
Jessica Bibby (11) 145

The Poems

A Day In The Life Of Charlie The Cat

Charlie wakes up
Eats
Goes outside
Does his business
And sleeps.

Charlie wakes up
Eats
Sprays the rug
Goes outside
And sleeps.

Charlie wakes up
Stays indoors
Plays around
Finds a cosy place
Eats and sleeps.

Charlie wakes up
Gets out of the window
Goes wild outside
Eats the grass
And sleeps.

Charlie wakes up
Looks for food
Moans for more
Gets his way
And sleeps.

Charlie gets in bed
Curls up
Closes his eyes
Purrs
And sleeps!

Louise Vickers (10)
Bishop Martin CE School, Woolton

Day In The Life Of Spotty The Rabbit

Spotty wakes up
Inspects the cage
Runs down her stairs
Eats
And sleeps!

Spotty wakes up
Does her business
Plays with her toys
Scratches herself
And sleeps!

Spotty wakes up
Bangs on her cage
Gets let out
Runs around the garden
Goes back in her cage
And sleeps!

Spotty wakes up
Drinks
Gets given grass and sweetcorn
Eats
And goes to bed.

Caurie-Jade Morgan (10)
Bishop Martin CE School, Woolton

Listen To Limericks

There once was a man called Bill
Who ate a dynamite pill
Off went his head
And it landed in bed
And his ears flew over the hill.

Erin Ellis (9)
Bishop Martin CE School, Woolton

The Starry Night

The three kings came from the East and were studying a bright star,
They went to Jerusalem, the journey was far.
They went to tell the King,
Herod wanted to do something.

He told the King to come back,
They were carrying a big, black sack.
Full of all the gifts for the new baby King,
Herod couldn't do anything.

The three kings set out to Bethlehem,
They were very tired because they'd already been to Jerusalem.
Then the star lay over the stable,
And near a table lay baby Jesus.

In a manger he lay,
The wise men stayed a long time.
They brought gifts of gold, frankincense and myrrh,
The shepherds brought only some sheep's fur.

They sang songs and praised the Lord,
No one was bored.
They stayed all night and all the next day,
Then the three kings quietly went away.

Stephen Lennox (9)
Bishop Martin CE School, Woolton

One Bright Star

Three wise men saw one bright star
Meaning a new king was born.
So they got gifts from lands afar
And travelled until it was morn.

When they found Herod he got really cross.
'Find him and bring him to me,' said the King,
In his mind he said, 'I am the boss!'
Then he said, 'Now I am the only king.'

They travelled to Bethlehem
And there in the hay
Lying before them
Baby Jesus lay.

They gave him myrrh, gold
and frankincense too.
Lord Jesus was cold
And went *atishoo!*

Emma Norris (10)
Bishop Martin CE School, Woolton

The Bright Star That Shone

In the east a bright star shone.
They knew that this one was the One!
The bright star was blinding
All the paths were made clear because they were winding.

The wise men were nearly crying
The journey was long and trying.
Desperate to get there
But where?

They saw the King
They told him about the newborn king.
Herod wanted to kill him
But the wise men ran and Herod said, 'I will win!'

They found a shed
Jesus wasn't lying in a bed.
They found Him lying in a manger
But baby Jesus was in danger.

Marley Davies (10)
Bishop Martin CE School, Woolton

The Best Gift

Three wise men and their camels
Travelling to see Jesus, with the animals.
First was Caspar, brave and bold,
And Jesus' gift from him, was glistening gold.

Next was Balthasar, giving myrrh,
As the sweet smell wafted through his camel's fur.
Melchior also, rode in night so dense.
Jesus Christ would have frankincense.

The gifts for Son of Mankind, of great expense,
Gold, myrrh and frankincense.
But the best gift for all three
Was seeing the sweet head of Thee.

Catrina Kenward (9)
Bishop Martin CE School, Woolton

The Seaside

Sun, heating
Waves, beating
Sea, splashing
Waves, crashing

> Umbrellas turning
> Children crying
> Some laughing
> Some smiling

Sandcastles small
Sandcastles tall
Ball throwing here
Ball throwing there
Ball throwing up and down
And everywhere.

Sara Ahmed (9)
Broadstone Hall Primary School, Stockport

My Journey To Ancient Egypt

E veryone is parched because of the glistening sun, beaming down on them.
G asping for breath, poor villagers are being forced to build the wealthy pharaoh's pyramids.
Y awning people row their boats down the long and slender river Nile as the sun comes up.
P eople are begging others for money or a small piece of food.
T alking and whispering amongst each other as the new pharaoh strolls by.

Jade Leishman (10)
Broadstone Hall Primary School, Stockport

Travel

T ravel on a bus, travel on a plane
R ow the boat 'til I see land
A fraid it might rain
V iewing the sea and sand
E scaping to the mainland
L ast but not least, I have to travel around.

Hannah Redfern (8)
Broadstone Hall Primary School, Stockport

The Karate Cat

There's a cat that knows karate,
There's a cat that knows kung-fu,
There's a cat that knows jujitsu,
And he's after me and you!

He draws with an old tooth,
He rubs out with his paw,
And if you try to hold his hand,
He'll flip you on the floor!

There's a cat that knows karate,
Who lives down Bosworth Street,
And here's a warning for you,
He's a cat you'd rather not meet!

Ellie Doyle (10)
Capenhurst CE Primary School, Capenhurst

Tropical Island

Tropical branches
Colourful sky
Dusty bush
Splashy sea
Shiny shore
Unbreakable coral
Goldfish sand
Coconut palms
Cold breeze
Squeaking parrots
Sea birds
Dripping salt
Juicy mangoes
Crumbling wave
Glistening atmosphere.

Abisaliny Arunprakash (10)
Castleway Primary School, Moreton

Tropical Island

See the . . .
Rough rocks
Bright sea
Tropical trees
Hot sand
Calm sea
Yellow sand
Empty view

Hear the . . .
Waves crashing
Trees swaying
Sand blowing
Parrots squawking

Smell the . . .
Beautiful coral
Salty water
Juicy coconuts.

Joel Barrow (9)
Castleway Primary School, Moreton

The Moon

Deep curves
Spread out
Wide open
Dark red and shiny gold
Clear, deep, black sky
Plain distance
Whistling breeze
Rough craters
Shivering cold
Dusty surface.

Jade Brereton-Weir (9)
Castleway Primary School, Moreton

Rainforest

Misty clouds
Foggy rain
Windy weather
Really hot
Hidden sky
Bushy trees
High trees
Bunched together
Often floods
Really colourful
Glisteningly wet
Squawking parrots
Noisy animals
Flowing river
Crackling thunder.

Kirsty Beaty (9)
Castleway Primary School, Moreton

Tropical Island

Hot sand
Tropical hill
Calm sea
Lovely sea
Dusty rocks
Tropical trees
No sand prints
Wide bay
Dry rocks
Calm, brilliant
Salty sea
Empty place
Islands.

Chloe Murphy (9)
Castleway Primary School, Moreton

Mountains

Slippery ice
Misty fog
Icy cold
Snowy white
Smoky clouds
Blue sky
Big points
Ripply slopes
Wavy curves
Hard climbing
Sharp danger
Pure white.

Megan Innes (9)
Castleway Primary School, Moreton

Antarctica

Cold breeze
Shivering edge
Cold body
Flaky waves
Sea sick
Pointy curves
Sharp tops
Long cracks
Big cracks
Striped blue
Calm bumps
Shadow, sky.

Sophie Maughan (10)
Castleway Primary School, Moreton

The Moon

Barren world
Bumpy craters
Dark shadows
Rocky plains
Beautiful sight
Bouncing high
Deafening silence
No oxygen
Dry place
Plantless land.

Bethany Price (9)
Castleway Primary School, Moreton

Thinking Of You

Thinking of you
In a special way
Is the way I do
Every day.

Jessica Handley (9)
English Martyrs RC Primary School, Litherland

My Nana!

My nana is a midget
She is the smallest digit
She cleans all day
And never stays away
When she puts on make-up
She makes me throw up
But when she's nice she's as cool as ice!

Berfim Katranbayiri
Gainsborough Junior School, Crewe

Sunny Day!

Today is a sunny day
I don't have to go to school
I'm going to play today
People think that's cool.

Today is a sunny day
I'm getting extremely hot
I'll get an orange juice
I'll like that a lot.

Today is a sunny day
My friends are coming over
I'll give them ice cream
One friend comes from Dover.

Today is a sunny day
I'm walking my Labrador
I'll go to the forest
Watching out for that chopped log.

Today is a sunny day
I'll have lots of fun
I'll have to do all this stuff
Before the day is done.

Today was a sunny day
It's getting quite dark
I wonder what we will do tomorrow
We may go to the park.

Paige Leek & Shuhro Mahmud
Gainsborough Junior School, Crewe

Dear Her Majesty

I once wrote a letter to Her Majesty the Queen
Asking her politely, would she like to come for tea?

The very next day I could see her reply,
Sitting on my doormat, out the corner of my eye.

I tore it from its envelope, it looked so fine,
The Queen says, 'Yes, just name your time!'

I couldn't believe my eyes, the Queen's coming round!
I wonder what she's like, might she wear her crown?

But I don't know what to cook; I don't know what she'd eat!
She might be a vegetarian or she might like meat.

I asked the Queen to supper, now I'm all confused,
We're going to go to Pizza Hut and that will have to do!

Isobelle Cooper
Gainsborough Junior School, Crewe

Gainsborough!

I love Gainsborough
It's safe, smiley and smart,
I've learnt how to work with numbers,
Read, write and art,
The dinners are healthy,
The teachers are great
And I get to play with my best mates,
The rules are simple,
The uniform is blue,
You get rewards for the things you do,
Gainsborough's the best;
I think it's great,
We start at 8.45am so don't be late!

Andraya Ball (10)
Gainsborough Junior School, Crewe

All About Dogs

Dogs are fun on a rainy day,
They will stay inside with you and play.
Our dog helps out with blind man's buff,
He knows he cannot be too rough.

And dogs are faithful, as you know;
They'll follow wherever you go.
To field and forest or by the sea,
Your dogs may keep you company.

Then dogs just love to give you a lick,
And they might even learn a trick!
Yes, day to day beginning to end,
They will always be your very best friend.

Bethan Lewsley
Gainsborough Junior School, Crewe

Snowman!

Snowmen dance around the land
Even on the ice and ground
If you will find the secret train
It will lead you to fame!

Tayniah Benson
Gainsborough Junior School, Crewe

Myself

My eyes are as brown as bear's fur.
My hair is as bright as the sun in the sky.
My teeth gleam like the moon.
My face twinkles, like a star from very far.
My eyelashes are as long as spider's legs.
That is me.

Libby Graham (8)
Halsnead Community Primary School, Whiston

Your Special Day!

Today is a special day
For my mum and dad,
So there is no need
To get stressed and mad.

Today is a special day
To put on your pretty dress,
Here comes the photographer,
He's part of the press.

Today is a special day,
Here comes the car,
Thankfully the church
Isn't very far.

Today is a special day,
Here comes the bride,
Look at my dad,
He's bursting with pride.

Today is a special day,
There are promises made,
Rings exchanged,
Your love will never fade.

Today is a special day,
I'll tell you the reason why,
Get your hankies ready,
I think you're going to cry.

Today is a special day,
Get out the knife,
Cut the cake,
Congratulations, man and wife.

Today is a special day,
So let's all raise a toast,
To two very special people,
Who I love the most!

Chloe Liderth (10)
Halsnead Community Primary School, Whiston

Halloween

Halloween has arrived,
Whilst we're running outside,
Ghostly ghouls are swooping out,
'Trick or treat,' the children shout!

Witches' shadows fly across the moon,
The midnight hour must be soon,
My outfit was as black as pitch,
Can you guess? I'm a wicked witch.

Spirits and souls come out at night,
Be careful they may want a fight,
They could wrap around you and take you away,
You'll have to be very careful today!

Children run and rush about,
Then they give a gleeful shout,
As the treats come rolling in,
Don't forget, wrappers in the bin!

Creepy crawlies, under your bed,
Witches flying up ahead,
Finally, at last it's night,
Don't let the bed bugs bite!

Cerys McStein-Roberts (10)
Halsnead Community Primary School, Whiston

Summer - Haikus

The sun has come out
To play from behind the clouds
Children are happy.

It is a bright day
The sun is shining brightly
A fine, clear day.

It is a hot day
The dull clouds have gone away
It is colourful.

Children are playing
Children out for a picnic
Children eating food.

Alicia Harrison (9)
Halsnead Community Primary School, Whiston

What Am I?

I have a long nose
I am very slow
I am a vegetarian
And I plod everywhere I go
I am very clever at swimming
I don't have any memory
I am wrinkly
I am always upset and in danger
Although I'm getting very old
I can break trees down if they are in my way
I'm not afraid of lions
Or any predator that attacks me.

Danielle Pickering (9)
Halsnead Community Primary School, Whiston

What Is The Sun?

It's a bright red boulder rolling through an ocean of clouds.
It's the golden eyeball of God, watching us.
It's a burning pumpkin, above the sapphire sky.
It's the story of suns, above a page of clouds.
It's a fiery defender of the star kingdom.
It's a fierce animal at the space zoo with its food . . . meteors!
It's the leader of all stars - soon they too will evolve.
It's the galaxy's clock ticking time away.
The shroud of all planets and the universe.

Marley Dwyer (10)
Halsnead Community Primary School, Whiston

Who Am I?

I am a girl
I play for Whiston Juniors
I've won a trophy six times
I also play for technique soccer
I've got three players of the day
I like football and my best teams are Liverpool and England
My best two players are Gerrard and Torres
I have green eyes and blonde hair
Who am I?

Megan Lee (8)
Halsnead Community Primary School, Whiston

River Of Love

Love is like a river
Flowing through our veins,
From our head to our toes, our love for each other grows,
Because you and I are meant to be together.

Katie Thompson (9)
Halsnead Community Primary School, Whiston

Silent

Walking through the silent mist
Cold and shivering
Walking through the silent mist
Scared and shocked
Walking through the silent mist
Troubled and upset
Walking through the silent mist
'Will we ever get home?'

Zachary Edmondson (9)
Halsnead Community Primary School, Whiston

What Is The Sun?

It is a scarlet clock, ticking away on a navy wall.
It is a shining ruby bead, floating on a tranquil sapphire sea.
It is a golden button lying on an aqua blanket.
It is an amber pumpkin squatting on a crystal blue carpet.
It is a scorching hot, carmine red ball, flaming on a piece of cobalt paper.
It is a burgundy bauble dangling from the azure ceiling.
It is an ochre plate hovering over an indigo table cloth.

Chloë J Nelson (10)
Halsnead Community Primary School, Whiston

Travelling Around The World With My Friends

My friend Molly, her nickname is Dolly,
But don't forget Heather, she is as light as a feather,
But my name is Sophie and my nickname is Dophie,
All of us are travelling around the world to Africa.

Sophie Richardson (7)
Halsnead Community Primary School, Whiston

Myself

My name is Heather
And I'm as light as a feather
I've got a friend called Erin May
And Ellie likes jelly
My favourite colour is blue, I like purple too
I've got a rabbit, her name is Fudgie
Her nickname is Budgie
I have some fish, some of them are as flat as a dish.

Heather Beesley (7)
Halsnead Community Primary School, Whiston

Birthday

Today
It's my birthday
It will be fun for me
And I am having a party
It's great!

Amy Tegg (9)
Halsnead Community Primary School, Whiston

Flowers

They bloom
All day, all night
Red, purple, blue and bright
The petals are beautiful and light
Forever.

Chloe Nicole Carmichael (9)
Halsnead Community Primary School, Whiston

My Animal

Today my happy dog
Has lumps on him that bleed
He has a bandage on him now
Poor dog.

Amy Cinnamond (9)
Halsnead Community Primary School, Whiston

A Summer Day

A nice sunny day
Children are playing with toys
The bright sun shining.

Kieran Leather (9)
Halsnead Community Primary School, Whiston

Snowy - Haiku

Snowballs being thrown
Snowman being made by kids
Cars frozen solid.

Daniel Bates (9)
Halsnead Community Primary School, Whiston

Spring - Haiku

Butterflies flying
Daffodils growing on grass
I like a spring day.

Laylah Scott (9)
Halsnead Community Primary School, Whiston

The Wives Of Henry VIII

Henry VIII was a big, fat king
From his first wife he got a ring
Katherine of Aragon was number one
Henry wanted to have a son.

Anne Boleyn was number two
Henry wanted to boil her in stew
One thing we can't understand
She had six fingers on one hand!

Jane Seymour was number three
She gave him a son, who she wanted to be
A king like Henry - big and fat
Then she dropped dead and that was that!

Anne of Cleves was number four
Who Henry wanted to adore
They gave their marriage a right good try
But sadly Henry said, 'Bye-bye.'

Catherine Howard was number five
But sadly she did not survive
She was sent to the tower, very sad
And knew that the news was horribly bad.

Number six was Catherine Parr -
The most successful wife, by far
She begged for mercy - she had faith
And these were the wives of Henry VIII.

Ewan Herd (7)
Ladymount RC School, Wirral

Archaeologist's Discovery

Archaeologist's discovery
Is a treasure recovery,
Diamonds and treasure are lovely together,
Unfortunately I have to dig forever!
Skeletons and bones, those are very old,
Good to look at, never sold.
Dirt and mud,
The job is understood,
Money and money, oh I love it!
When I discover it,
Rubies, big and vast,
Roman jewellery from the past.

Millie Bolton (9)
Newton Bank Preparatory School, Newton-le-Willows

Time Travel To The Past And Future

Once I went to the past,
I saw a dinosaur, big and vast,
I saw the Tudors,
They were feuders.

Once, to the future I went,
I saw a robot, he was rusty and bent,
I saw new kings and queens,
They were not mean.

Who knows what tomorrow will bring,
Maybe even a diamond ring.

Charlotte Crook (10)
Newton Bank Preparatory School, Newton-le-Willows

Under The Sea

What bright colours, blinding me,
When I look under the sea,
Diving deep down and down,
What's that fish, is it a clown?
Over there it's very dark,
I wonder if I'll see a shark,
A stingray is frying his treats for lunch,
I can hear his bones going *crunch, crunch, crunch,*
Seaweed, slimy and green,
And then I woke and it was all a dream!

Tayler Brown (10)
Newton Bank Preparatory School, Newton-le-Willows

Usain Bolt

Really fast,
Sprinting expert,
Running champion,
Brilliantly speedy,
Record setter,
Amazing man,
Very fit,
Really muscular,
Jamaican champion,
Super quick.

Nikhil Mediratta (8)
Newton Bank Preparatory School, Newton-le-Willows

Firefly

Night creature,
Soft bodied,
Colourful light,
Flying quickly,
Flying high,
Up above,
Yellow wings,
Sky bugs,
Loud noises,
Four wings.

Zarah Mughal (9)
Newton Bank Preparatory School, Newton-le-Willows

Squirrel

Nut muncher,
Fluffy tail,
Food hider,
Furry friend,
Birdfeeder raider,
Tree climber,
Mouse spy,
Pricked-up ears,
Twitching whiskers,
Acorn gobbler.

Iona Molyneaux Townshend (8)
Newton Bank Preparatory School, Newton-le-Willows

Ant Eater

Curly tongue,
Endless tail,
Enormous ears,
Short legs,
Gigantic body,
Huge eyes,
Brown-grey,
Termite loving,
Rainforest dwelling,
Hairy snout!

Darren Bettany (7)
Newton Bank Preparatory School, Newton-le-Willows

Homer Simpson

Doughnut lover,
Fat man,
Food fanatic,
Beer worshipper,
Couch potato,
Church hater,
Champion dribbler,
Underpants man,
Yellow dude,
Bowling champion.

Finnley Shufflebotham (8)
Newton Bank Preparatory School, Newton-le-Willows

Under The Sea

Under the sea,
Is where I want to be,
Under the sea,
The fish swimming around me,
Under the sea,
Stingrays swimming away from me,
Then the shark,
Comes out at dark,
Under the sea,
What a wonderful place to be.

Charlie Morris (10)
Newton Bank Preparatory School, Newton-le-Willows

A Barn Owl

White chest,
Speckled wings,
Soundless flight,
Twistable neck,
Mouse supper,
Curved beak,
Hooked claws,
Fearsome predator,
Hoot, hoot.

Rosie Robinson (9)
Newton Bank Preparatory School, Newton-le-Willows

Cheshire & Merseyside

Time Travel Adventure

I start off in 2010
Then I end up in 1920!
I try pressing the button and . . .
Zoom!
Now I am in the year 3000!
Oh what does this do . . .
Whoosh!
Uh oh, I am in the stone age
I sat down and waited
'When can I go back to 2010?'
How I miss it, if only I hadn't gone in the time machine!
Then an idea shot into my head
I'll just press this up in years button until 2010
1997, 1998, 1999, 2000, 2001. 2002 . . .
2010!
I could have jumped for joy
Oh, where have I landed?
Don't say it's . . . next door's garden"!

Olivia Davies (9)
Our Lady of Pity RC Primary School, Wirral

Up, Up And Away

Up, up and away
It's like a little holiday
It's a ride
It's so fun
When I'm scared
I say, 'What shall I dooo?'
When I'm so high
I say, 'Where am I?'
Sometimes we have an accident
Sometimes we go down and we go upside down.

Molly Nelson
Our Lady of Pity RC Primary School, Wirral

Time Travel

Time, time, time
Travel is so quick
It's like lightning, it's handy and cool
I love what it can do
It's interesting
I loved time travel when it was invented
One day you will too
Tomorrow, just a minute away
Because time travel is so quick
I love it, you will too
One day
Time, time, time travel.

Melissa Heller (8)
Our Lady of Pity RC Primary School, Wirral

Under The Sea

Under the sea,
The deep, deep sea,.
A hustle,
A bustle,
Swish, swash, swoosh,
An octopus,
A rainbow fish,
Wow, what can I see?
A rainbow,
A eight-legged creature,
What can you see?

Isobella Cromby-While (9)
Our Lady of Pity RC Primary School, Wirral

Archaeologists

Archaeologists dig for hidden pottery.
They have big shovels!
They also have huge axes.
They are hard working
And found Tutankhamun.
Oh, you're wonderful.
Archaeologists, how do you do it?
I admire you so much.

Andrew Walsh (8)
Our Lady of Pity RC Primary School, Wirral

My Favourite Place

We use the garden as a jungle.
In the summer we have a water fight.
Her dad's got a truck that we have a snack in.
We play the army game and make obstacles.
We slide down the big, green tank and climb up it again.
I miss my friend!

Anya Brown (8)
Our Lady of Pity RC Primary School, Wirral

When I Met An Archaeologist

When I met the archaeologist who was digging up jewels and bones,
It was very strange when I met him because his name was Mr Jones.
He dug up fossils and bits of gold,
He is very strong this Mr Jones, very big and bold.
He gave me diamonds, emeralds and ruby,
Then suddenly he took out a stereo and started to boogie.

Rachel Holland (9)
Our Lady of Pity RC Primary School, Wirral

Up, Up And Away

Kites, balloons
Lift me up
Up, into the sky
What can I do
When I'm so high?

Mathew Lightfoot (7)
Our Lady of Pity RC Primary School, Wirral

Mermaid Kennings

Swimming racer
Human looker

Tail flapper
Water breather

Sea creature
Party goer

Bubble rusher
Fish lover

Wave racer
Cave liver

Music lover
Love changer

Mer-brother
Trouble catcher

Land lover.

Ellen Cook (8)
Our Lady Star of the Sea Primary School, Seaforth

Michael Jackson's Lullaby

Hush little Jacko, don't you cry!
Ryan's going to get you a star from the sky.

And if that star doesn't shine,
Ryan's going to get you a glass of wine.

And if that wines makes you drunk,
Ryan's going to get you a new pet skunk.

And if that skunk is too smelly,
Ryan's going to get you a bright red jelly.

And if that jelly makes you fat,
Ryan's going to get you a new pet rat.

And if that rat's name is Ben,
Ryan's going to take you to the lion's den.

And if that lion's den's in France,
Ryan's going to teach you how to dance.

And if that dance makes you squawk,
Ryan's going to teach you the moonwalk.

And if that moonwalk hurts your toes,
Ryan's going to get you a plastic nose.

And if that nose lets you down,
You'll still be the best Jacko in Motown.

Ryan Thurlbeck (9)
Our Lady Star of the Sea Primary School, Seaforth

Mary, Mary

Mary, Mary went down town,
Showing off her silver crown.
It wasn't that fantastic,
It was just made out of plastic!

Caitlin Rose Eileen Mullin (8)
Our Lady Star of the Sea Primary School, Seaforth

My Cat

My cat, Purdy
She plays all day!
She's very fussy about her food
She's always in a grumpy mood.
She's always fighting with her friends
And if she doesn't get her own way
She will go outside and play!
Her best friend is Smudge
Who is very shy
But that's enough to say for now,
So bye-bye!

Emily Moore (8)
Our Lady Star of the Sea Primary School, Seaforth

Running

Muddy shoes!
Every race leaves muddy footprints
Wherever you go.
In big races you come in
Four hundred and fiftieth place.
In small races you come first
Or 'last but not least'.
In medium races you come second.
Go home and wash those muddy feet!

Conor Donnelly (9)
Our Lady Star of the Sea Primary School, Seaforth

Chocolate

Chocolate milkshake
Shake, shake, shake
Chocolate cake
Bake, bake, bake
Chocolate bar
Yummy in my tummy!
Eat it all up, but o-oh!
I've got tummy ache!

Jack Moore (8)
Our Lady Star of the Sea Primary School, Seaforth

My Dog

She plays tug of war
She mostly wins
But I win sometimes
Mostly she is hungry
And she always eats
No matter what it is!

Ryan Quinn (9)
Our Lady Star of the Sea Primary School, Seaforth

Rabbit

R uns and eats
A mazingly fast
B ites toys
B abies are born in a house under the ground
I tchy, scratchy
T reats are played with.

Mia Shaw (8)
Our Lady Star of the Sea Primary School, Seaforth

Dog

D igging for bones
O n the garden lawn
G uarding and protecting.

Dylan Gibney (8)
Our Lady Star of the Sea Primary School, Seaforth

Friend Or Foe?

Freezing cold temperatures; gases in the air,
Animals are dying, does anyone care?

Can you bear the sight of a polar bear,
When it's hungry, sick and poor?
When global warming has killed the world?
We can't have it anymore.

Mother Earth was smiling a long time ago,
Now she's sad and frowning,
She has lost her glow.

Blooming flowers,
Trees so tall,
Birds start to die,
We will lose them all!

Factories smoke,
As the world starts to choke,
Beauty will fade,
From the mistakes we've made!

We can change the world,
In a matter of days,
By lowering car fumes
There's a lot of different ways!

Holly Kitchingman (11)
Our Lady's Catholic Primary School, Warrington

Whose Side Are You On?

Mother Earth is sad,
Please make her glad.
Mother Nature is crying,
Her animals are dying.

Because of the fumes,
The flowers don't bloom.
Global warming is killing,
The animals so thrilling.

Please save your home,
And do not moan.
We have caused this mess,
She's in distress.

Ashamed of her children,
And what they have done.
The sun has won the prize,
The sun has won.

The prize for the nastiest,
The prize for the meanest,
Showing off because he is the cleanest,
The Earth is dirty now, oh what a shame
And we are to blame.

Save the world!
Be a hero!
And make the North Pole
Go back to sub-zero!

She has no one on her side,
Please decide.
Please be her friend
Or she will end!

Ruby-Rose McGann (10)
Our Lady's Catholic Primary School, Warrington

Mother Earth

What is Mother Earth?
Mother Earth is the green fields
And the animals that live on them.
But if we carry on
No more green fields,
No more animals.

What is Mother Earth?
Mother Earth is the sea,
Lakes and the rivers.
But if we carry on,
Her waters will drain,
Such a shame, what a pain.

What is Mother Earth?
Mother Earth is her wealthy, healthy children,
Polluting her beauty,
Making her cry, and die.

What is Mother Earth?
Mother Earth is a clock;
Time is running out,
Counting down.
Will you save Mother Earth?

Tyra Hamblett (10)
Our Lady's Catholic Primary School, Warrington

Mother Nature

People crying, animals dying,
Our earth sighing,
To get their nature back
That has been stolen!
Ice has started to melt and the Arctic has felt
The sadness of their homes being destroyed
And they will be annoyed.
We won't let this fail again,
And won't let our world become a flame.
Please Mother Nature, don't come to an end,
Because we will always be
Your most loving, best friend!
Animals should be free as they travel,
They will see you, Mother Nature keep on trying
And you may not have failure.
The things they steal
They don't give back,
So we should be ready for attack.
Mother Nature please keep strong,
Sing your song,
Never give in, because you know
Global warming won't cure their sin!

Lydia Smith (10)
Our Lady's Catholic Primary School, Warrington

Global Fear

Do you care?
It's such a scare,
Global warming is happening!
And we are helping
What does it do?
Chimneys, choking,
People, polluting,
Animals, crying,
Nature, dying.

The Earth is crying
With excruciating pain
Her face is being shaved of grass and green
Do you care?
Does anyone care?

So start playing
And do your part.
Life might not end
If you're Earth's friend.

Ben Tavlin (11)
Our Lady's Catholic Primary School, Warrington

Are You Earth's Friend?

What is global warming?
What does it do?
It's killing Mother Nature
All the wildlife too.
Her face is being shaved clean
With excruciating pain.
Do you really care?

People polluting,
Chimneys smoking,
Factories choking,
Gas polluting.

What are you going to do?
Save all the polar bears,
Animals and Mother Earth.
Start playing it smart
And do your part.
Life might not end
If you're Earth's friend.

Sharna Boyle
Our Lady's Catholic Primary School, Warrington

What Will Happen?

What about the trees?
They will all go.
What about the polar bears?
What about their snow?
We are the polluters of our Earth,
Nobody knows how much it's worth.
Does anybody really care
About the world we all share?
Fumes and littering,
All this is global warming.
Our world is burning constantly.
All of this is because of you and me.
Global warming is the fear of the planet,
It is the fear of all who live on it.
Our future is in our hands,
We can stop the destruction of lands.
Life might not end
If you're Earth's friend.

Daniel Marsh (10)
Our Lady's Catholic Primary School, Warrington

Global Warming

Our planet Earth is precious and can't be replaced,
We need to act now or our homes will be erased.
Burning temperatures, more gases in our air,
Overflowing and hurting Mother Nature, does anyone really care?

Leaves will become brown,
Then everyone will frown,
Time is counting down and running out,
So look after our world and stop the drought.

Global warming is not cool, so stop being a fool,
Because of the fumes no blossoms will bloom.
Life might not end if you are Earth's friend,
To animals and plants,
Earth would be under a trance.

Sophie Logan (11)
Our Lady's Catholic Primary School, Warrington

Global Warming

Are you Earth's friend?
Do you care if Mother Earth is crying,
And all the animals are dying?
Are you Earth's friend?

Mother Earth burns with anger
What are you going to do?
Are you Earth's friend?

People polluting,
Chimneys smoking,
Nature dying.
What are you going to do?
Life might not end
If you're Earth's friend.

Brittany Leah (10)
Our Lady's Catholic Primary School, Warrington

Mother Earth

The world is spinning around
Time is counting down and running out.
For Mother Earth is crying,
Global warming, harming.

Chimneys smoking, people choking,
Global warming is harming Mother Earth,
Mother Nature cannot give birth.
Life might not end,
If you're Mother Earth's friend.

We are polluters, polluting,
Gases choking Mother Earth,
So start playing it smart,
And do your part!

Rebecca Savage (10)
Our Lady's Catholic Primary School, Warrington

Global Warming

Global warming, what a pain,
Tragedies happening, such a shame,
Toxic gases in the air,
But does anyone ever, really care?

Factories don't listen to what we say,
We face these things every day,
Animals face excruciating pain,
And all the plants are losing their fame.

We've got no water, we are weak,
And now everything just looks so bleak,
We have made Mother Earth so sad,
Now let's try to make her glad.

Andrew Smith (11)
Our Lady's Catholic Primary School, Warrington

Rainbow Fish Party

First a ripple
Then a fin
Lots of little waves on skin
Skimming softly, sweeping, slowly creeping
Jump! Splash!

Then a swirl, round and round
Skimming softly, swirling, faster, faster
Swirl! Splash!

Lastly, growing water flowing
Like a waterfall
Is it real?
Yes
It's a rainbow fish party!
*Splash! Swirl! Swish! Skim!
Oh! They're gone!*

Marian Eilidh Unwin (8)
Penketh Community Primary School, Penketh

The Old Man

Today I met an old man,
His beard was long and thin
He said he liked to stir up
Baked beans in a plastic tin
He had a moustache
I bet you do too
He had legs as big as bananas
Well, that is all I can say
For now!
Well bye-bye for now or as I say . . .
Hananasop Lecasrom!

Molly Weir (8)
Penketh Community Primary School, Penketh

Ghosts

Ghosts are creepy,
Ghosts are faint,
Ghosts are terrifying,
Ghosts are transparent,
Ghosts travel all the way through,
They come out at dark,
Watch out, they want vengeance,
Spirits haunt the town,
Haunting far above the ground
Haunting near to the ground
Oh!
It's time to meet your doom
Wahahaha!
Boo!

Abbie Taylor (8)
Penketh Community Primary School, Penketh

My Bedroom

My bedroom is a mess
But I think it's the best
You can't really complain
Because they're all the same!

My mum tells me to tidy up
When I always get fed up
But I always end up making a den
Like a chicken in a pen!

Okay, I admit I live in a pig sty
And have no room to play
Oh!
An idea popped into my head
I'll tidy it up the next day!

Faye McGrath (9)
Penketh Community Primary School, Penketh

That Is How We Do It

Mathew sang beautifully
Ruby smiled proudly
Harry talked interestingly
Jordan laughed skilfully
Morgan listened carefully
Bradleigh ate beautifully
And that is how we do it!

Tim snored lazily
Angela turned rudely
Logan burped loudly
Zoey wrote disgracefully
Michelle sang horribly
And that is how we do it!

Gemma Clarke (8)
Penketh Community Primary School, Penketh

Zombie Curse

A zombie marched down a street one night
Pushing who he saw
But when it became light he was a man again!

So stay inside, you will be safe
Don't go outside at night!

Listen to my warning
You won't regret it
What I have said!

He is black
And covered in blood
Eats what he sees
Don't go outside!

Matthew Wright (9)
Penketh Community Primary School, Penketh

Aliens

Aliens are extremely lazy
They are really weird
They have lots of funny toys
And I saw one that has a beard.

Aliens have at least three eyes
They make lots of noise
They love to scare and surprise
C'mon girls and boys.

Aliens are so cool
They love to play football
They love to rule the moon
And they're all silly.

Gabrielle Andrus (9)
Penketh Community Primary School, Penketh

Dragon

Once I met a dragon
A small and happy dragon
So I decided to put him
In my shiny red wagon.

The next day I saw that dragon
He was no longer small
His tail was long and big and strong
And very, very tall.

My best friend is that dragon
He is still here today
We do anything we want
And that is all I have to say.

Lee Robert Wilson (9)
Penketh Community Primary School, Penketh

So Do You!

Joe picks his nose
So do you!
Jamie has a paddy
And so do you!

Alex is lazy
So are you!
Jack is crazy
And so are you!

Fred is smart
So are you!
Sam is smelly
And so are you!

Courtney Swindell (8) & Molly Wooldridge (9)
Penketh Community Primary School, Penketh

Pop Stars

Pop stars
Pop stars
Pop stars
Sometimes they have to lie
When their concerts are cancelled
You know you have to cry.

Pop stars sometimes dance
Pop stars sometimes sing
Some of them DJ
'Yo, people wear bling!'

Tyler Westwood (9)
Penketh Community Primary School, Penketh

ABC

ABC come with me
You know you want
To play with me.

ABC come along
I am waiting for you
To sing a song.

ABC you're finally out
I want you to sing
Scream and shout.

Hannah Carver (8)
Penketh Community Primary School, Penketh

Cool Cat

Eye flutterer
Fur licker
Mouse muncher
Bird eater
Bed nicker
Fish scratcher
Whisker stroker
Tail slapper
Lap leaper.

Jordan Edge (8)
Penketh Community Primary School, Penketh

Fiddler, Fiddler

Fiddler, fiddler,
You and me
Make me a tune
For you and me
Make it fast
For half-past two
Because
I might be at
The zoo.

Jack Taylor (8)
Penketh Community Primary School, Penketh

I'm Gonna Throw Up!

Pirates puke on stormy seas
Giants spew on top of trees
Kings are sick in golden loos
Dogs vomit on Daddy's shoes.

Babies love to make a mess
Down the front of Mum's best dress
And what car ride would be complete
Without the stink of last night's treat.

Harry Bromwell (8)
Penketh Community Primary School, Penketh

My Bedroom

My bedroom is a mess
It is really not the best
It could be better than the rest
Girls like me are best
But my dress is a mess.

Rosie Burgess (9)
Penketh Community Primary School, Penketh

Snowball

S now is falling on the ground
N ow the children are playing around
O pen up your window
W atch the snowflakes flow
B oys are playing in the snow,
A ll the girls, as well
L aughing all the way
L apping up the snow all day.

Alexander Zachariah Winstanley-Venables (9)
Penketh Community Primary School, Penketh

Sky In The Pie

Wait, there is a sky in the pie,
Remove it at once, if you please,
You can keep your incredible sunsets
But I ordered mincemeat and cheese!

I can't stand nightingales singing,
With clouds all brushed with my
Gold!

Ellie Roberts (8)
Penketh Community Primary School, Penketh

Remember The Poppy Very Red

The soldiers that pray,
The soldiers that lay,
The soldiers lying in the mud,
Their arms and legs covered in blood.

The poor soldiers that have to die,
Their poor families that were left behind,
The poor soldiers covered in blood,
Adolf Hitler covered in blood.

Bombs dancing all around,
Making big craters in the ground,
The rain falling,
The tanks crawling.

Remember the poppy, very red,
Remember the soldiers without a bed,
So take two minutes of silence
To thank the ones that saved our lives.
Also remember the ones that lost their lives.
Lest we forget.

Lauryn Huxley (11)
Plantation Primary School, Halewood

Lest We Forget

The soldiers dying as bombs are dropping,
The soldiers flying through the air.
The mud trenches as red as poppy fields.

Aeroplanes diving from high above.
Aeroplanes beaming straight through the clouds,
Guns firing from every direction,
Bullets screeching right through the air.
Lest we forget.

James Horn (11)
Plantation Primary School, Halewood

Remember The Poppy Very Red

When the soldiers come marching through the blazing sun,
They know that there's worse to come.
When the colour of a poppy resembles the blood,
There he was, brave he stood.
So where's a poppy for their sake?
Don't let their sweet, brave hearts break.
They don't ask for much, just a little respect,
A two minutes silence, so don't forget.
When they have a cold or the flu
Wishing they don't get killed by an MG42.
Brave and bold as they stood,
When they scatter in that mud.
The soldiers, not knowing their children had been taken away,
Where they live, where they eat and where they stay.
In the war, where it's madness,
Astonishing gunshots, it all ends in sadness.
The Germans, yes who we beat,
The Germans had a destroying defeat.
That we bet,
Less we forget.

James Mullings (11)
Plantation Primary School, Halewood

Soldier's March

Soldiers march until their lives are reached.
We try to teach, but they will be beat.

But lives are always going to come to an end,
They come round a bend and their lives will come to a dead end.

Guns shooting, up and down, like the trusty Spitfire.
The death-toll of soldiers climbing, higher and higher.

Lest we forget the ones who died.

Ben Harper (10)
Plantation Primary School, Halewood

Lest We Forget

Remember, remember, 11th day of November,
The fallen brave young men of war.
Loved ones waiting patiently at the door.

Blood pouring out as a river of red,
Blood running down broken faces,
Bombs shouting from dark skies.

Bombs came down and danced all around.
Salute all soldiers who fought for our safety.
So buy yourself a poppy to show respect,
Lest we forget!

Rachael Kofoed (10)
Plantation Primary School, Halewood

Blood Pouring

Soldiers walking through the street,
Knowing they have not been beat.
They didn't give us any warning,
Soldiers dead in the morning.

Why did people die for this?
It's like falling down an endless abyss!

Bombs pouring like monsoon rain,
As the evacuees watch from the train.
Buildings blasted to the ground,
House shattered all around.

Lewis Green (11)
Plantation Primary School, Halewood

My Dream

The snow fell softly on my drive,
Covering the lush, green trees.

On the front step were my two gerbils,
Snuggled together,
Like they'd appeared out of nowhere.

Then they scurried towards me,
Fighting on their way there.
When their eyes locked on mine
It brought back happy memories.

I remembered how they used to relax on the couch,
Scratching each other in the bright light of the TV.
How I wish they could come back.

Dreaming of snow's a good omen they say
And to dream of snow in autumn foreshadows happiness . . .

I'd dream an avalanche if it brought back my gerbils.

Millicent Mae Lawlor (9)
Plantation Primary School, Halewood

The Hedgehog

(Based on the book by Dick King-Smith)

Max is a brave hedgehog,
He is very spiky,
He is smart and very kind,
He's got a pointy, black nose.

Max is a curious boy,
He's brown all over,
Max loves eating slugs,
He is a very funny hedgehog,
He is a determined hedgehog.

Holly Mulhearn (9)
Plantation Primary School, Halewood

Men In Battle

We all stood together in battle,
Just like cows and cattle.
I ducked down to take a breath,
When I turned around there was nothing to see but death.
The smoke spreading through the land,
When it hit, it was coughing and pouring out like sand.

I heard a strange voice in my ear,
Then I noticed the Nazis were near,
When I turned around
All of my friends were on the ground.

As the mud pulled me down,
Bombs, dancing, fell to the ground.
Take a moment to remember me,
So buy yourself a red poppy.

James Higham (10)
Plantation Primary School, Halewood

I'm The Person

I'm the person you left alone,
I'm the person whose heart went cold.
The kicking, the hitting, there's so much pain,
I'm the person you left in strain.
I don't want to go to school because you'll hurt me again.

I'm the person who sat in bed worrying you'd strike again.
I'm the person who cries themselves to sleep.
I'm the person who never will speak!

I'm the person who suffers every day,
I'm the person who never will play.

You push me, you kick me, you make me cry,
Then I think, *Who am I?*

Eleanor Stock (9)
Plantation Primary School, Halewood

Remember Me, Red Poppy

We're all standing together in battle,
Just like cows and cattle,
I ducked down to take a breath,
When I turned around there was nothing to see but death.
The smoke hurtling throughout the land,
When it hit is was coughing and pouring out like sand.

I heard a strange voice in my head,
But then, I'm nearly dead,
When I walked backwards I fell to the ground,
Then I looked; it was my friend's dead body in the sand.
As the mud pulled us down,
The bombs came dancing to the ground.
Take a moment to remember me
And buy yourself a red poppy.

Elliot Fewtrell (10)
Plantation Primary School, Halewood

Remember, Remember The 11th Day Of November

Remember, remember, the 11th day of November,
The fallen, brave young men of war,
Loved ones waiting patiently at the door.

Blood pouring out as a river of red,
Blood running down broken faces,
Bombs shouting down from dark skies.

Bombs come down and dance all around,
So salute the soldiers who fought for our safety,
Buy yourself a poppy to show your respect.

> Lest we forget,
> Remember us!

Caitlin Lloyd (11)
Plantation Primary School, Halewood

Lest We Forget

The soldiers that pray,
The soldiers that lay,
The soldiers living in mud,
Their arms and legs covered in blood.

The poor soldiers that have to die,
Their poor families that were left behind,
The poor soldiers covered in blood,
Adolf Hitler covered in blood.

Bombs dancing all around,
Making big craters in the ground,
The rain falling,
The tanks crawling.

Remember the poppy, very red,
Remember the soldiers without a bed,
So take two minutes of silence
To thank the soldiers that saved our lives.
To thank the soldiers that lost their lives.
Lest we forget.

Alexandra Greenwood (10)
Plantation Primary School, Halewood

The Battlefield

The blood crept up my throat as my end was nigh,
The rain crashed into us, but still I will not die.
The battlefield suffocated under the weight,
Bullets drove past, deciding people's fate,
The grenades murdered us, as they flew in.
Lightning punched into us like a pin,
Twisted, the trees stood tall.
Fire was cooking and it wouldn't fall.
This is my battlefield.

Adam Smith (11)
Plantation Primary School, Halewood

I Am The Person You Bullied At School

I am the person you bullied at school,
I am the person that wasn't cool,
I am the person who walked alone,
I am the person that's scared going home.
I am the person that always gets hit
I am the person covered in spit,
I am the person being waited for,
I am the person rated poor.
I am the person that everyone hated,
I am the person really frustrated.
I am the person that wears goofy glasses,
I am the person who cries during classes.
I am the person that deserves to be cool too,
I am a person just like *you!*

Ryan McCrae (10)
Plantation Primary School, Halewood

Haunted House

I am the ghost of the evil past,
Once I had my arm in a bright blue cast.
I live in a haunted house,
Bright blue and green,
No wonder I keep it clean.

In the garden, trees stand to attention,
My kids in school don't do detention.

Windows whistled,
Sun shone,
Flowers dashed.

All this in the haunted house!

Sophie Baugh (10)
Plantation Primary School, Halewood

Blood Street

Blood pouring,
Soldiers walking through the street,
Knowing they have not been beat,
They didn't give us any warning,
Soldiers died in the morning.

Why did people die for this?
It's like falling down an endless abyss,
Bombs fall like monsoon rain,
As evacuees watch from the train.

Buildings blasted to the ground,
Houses shattered all around.

Jack Gargan (11)
Plantation Primary School, Halewood

Battlefield

The soldiers suffering with the roaring fire,
The flames laughing as they get higher and higher.
The gunshots dancing and passing the soldiers by,
But in a few minutes they might just die.

Gunshots running around the trenches,
They don't have time to sit on benches . . .
The power of the gun makes then want to run and run.

As they get ready to fight on the battlefield,
They get ready to write -
                That they fought.
                Lest we forget.

Aaron Ellis (10)
Plantation Primary School, Halewood

Remember Me

We're all standing together in battle,
Just like cows and cattle.
I ducked down to take a breath,
When I turned around there nothing to see but death.

I heard a strange voice in my ear,
Then I knew the Nazis were near,
When I turned around
All I saw was my friend on the ground.

As the mud pulled the soldiers down,
The bombs came dancing down and fell to the ground.
Take a moment to remember me and buy yourself a red poppy.

Megan Humphreys (11)
Plantation Primary School, Halewood

The Soldiers

The soldiers dying, as bombs are dropping,
The soldiers flying through the air.
The mud trenches as blood-red as poppy fields.
Aeroplanes diving from high above,
Aeroplanes beaming straight through the clouds,
Guns firing, like aeroplanes flying.

Guns giving nearly everybody an infection,
Guns firing from every direction.
Bullets screeching tight through the air.

Lest we forget!

Owen Mulhearn (10)
Plantation Primary School, Halewood

Remember, Remember

Remember, remember, 11th day of November,
The fallen brave young men of war.
Loved ones waiting patiently at the door.

Blood pouring out as a river of red,
Blood running down broken faces,
Bombs shouting from dark skies.

Bombs came down and danced all around.
So salute all soldiers who fought for our safety.
So buy yourself a poppy to show respect,
Lest we forget!

Lydia Stratulis (10)
Plantation Primary School, Halewood

The Trusty Spitfire

Soldiers march until their lives are reached,
We try and reach but they will be beat.
Lives are always going to come to an end,
They come round a bend and there their lives will come to an end.

Guns shooting up and down,
Like the trusty Spitfire,
The death toll of soldiers
Climbing higher and higher.

Lest we forget the ones that died,
The red poppies in the battlefield, diving lower and lower.

Abbie McHugh (11)
Plantation Primary School, Halewood

Gunshots

The soldiers suffering,
With the laughing fire,
The flames laugh as they get higher and higher.
The gunshots running past the soldiers,
But in a few minutes they might die.

Gunshots running around the trenches,
They don't have time to sit on benches.
The power of the gun
Makes them want to run and run
As they get ready to fight in the battle.

Arron Muirhead (10)
Plantation Primary School, Halewood

The Tanks

I look at each and every corner,
All I see are lifeless bodies flying up into the sky.
As the dancing flames wave in the sky,
The tanks crawled towards us.
The soldiers marching to attention, the mud shot at their feet,
The bullets propelled in to the sky,
Like a helicopter flying straight ahead.
The soldiers fighting as the guns dance in their hands.
Poppy Day, Poppy Day -
Remember those who died.

Jennifer Edwards (10)
Plantation Primary School, Halewood

The Hodgeheg

(Based on the book by Dick King-Smith)

Max is a very brave hedgehog,
He is brown and spiky,
Max is smart and kind,
He is a determined hedgehog.

Max is a curious little boy,
He has got a pointy, black nose,
Max likes eating slimy slugs,
He is a funny hedgehog.

Karla Jordan (9)
Plantation Primary School, Halewood

Bullets In Their Backs

Tanks roaring with bombs,
Bullets screeching through the air,
Blood pouring like a waterfall,
When the bouncing bombs came tumbling down,
People screamed and ran around.

Men shook with bullets in their backs,
Nazis came with a fierce attack.
Bombs diving through the air,
Now people are dying everywhere.

Nathan Williams (10)
Plantation Primary School, Halewood

Bombs Diving

Tanks roaring with bombs,
Bullets screeching through the air,
Blood pouring like a waterfall,
When the bouncing bombs came tumbling down,
People screamed and ran around.

Men shook with bullets in their backs,
Nazis came with a fierce attack,
Bombs diving from the air,
Now people are dying everywhere.

Lauryn Goulding (10)
Plantation Primary School, Halewood

The Hodgeheg
(Based on the book by Dick King-Smith)

Max, the hedgehog, is very brave,
Max is funny, getting his words mixed up.
Max is very kind,
He likes to eat fat, slimy worms.

He is a very spiky hedgehog.
He is very determined,
Max is very smart,
Max is very loving.

James Critchley (8)
Plantation Primary School, Halewood

The Hodgeheg
(Based on the book by Dick King-Smith)

Max is very brave and determined,
He is small and spiky,
He is small but smart.

He is cautious about the road,
He likes fat, slimy worms.
He likes worms and slugs.
This sounds very strange, but he likes dog food too.

Jamie Andrews (9)
Plantation Primary School, Halewood

We Reach A Dead End

Soldiers march until their lives are reached.
We try to teach, but they will be beat.

Lives are always going to come to an end,
They come round a bend and their lives will come to a dead end.

Guns shooting, up and down, like the trusty Spitfire.
The death-toll of soldiers climbing, higher and higher.

Lest we forget the ones who died.

Bethany Smith (10)
Plantation Primary School, Halewood

Untitled

Yellow lumpy custard,
Green snot pie,
All mixed together
With a dead dog's eye.
Slap it on a buttie,
Nice and thick
And swallow it down
With a cold cup of sick!

Lauren Owen (10)
Plantation Primary School, Halewood

Blood Pouring

Blood pouring -
Soldiers walking through the street
Knowing they have not been beat.

Why did people die for this?
It's like falling down an endless abyss.

Bombs poring like monsoon rain,
Evacuees watched from the train.

George Panther (10)
Plantation Primary School, Halewood

Snow Poem

Snow is a white wonderland
A child's best friend
Soft as a feather, cold as ice
Snowball fights, sledging races
All of these things add up to a lot of fun
Snow down your neck, frozen hands
All of these things are not so fun.

Harry Aldrich & Lucy Wilkinson
Prestbury CE Primary School, Prestbury

What Is Snow?

What is snow?
Now you'll know.

Soft winter blankets cover the ground,
Pitter patter, drops the snow all around.

Joyful children play in the winter wonderland,
Feeling as if the snow were crunchy sand.

Trees so beautiful, they blind your eyes,
Skies so blue, they tell surprising lies.

Winter's animals roam the frozen ground,
Searching for sumptuous food all around.

Children in their puffy suits,
Matching coat and comfy boots.

Sledging down the icy slopes,
Before spring comes to melt their snowy hopes.

**Emma Crook (9), Lauren Gardner (9)
& Sam Lawson (10)**
Prestbury CE Primary School, Prestbury

Autumn

Autumn is like a feathery,
hazel bird, gliding through the funeral of the sun.
He is a russet fire settling in a twig-filled ditch.
He is a brassy, glassy plane,
nesting in the centre of a yellow, freckly tree.
Autumn is a moist teardrop,
flowing down into the misty stream meandering through the wood.
He is a shooting star,
soaring into a murky fog, glinting ever so slightly.
He is a tawny arrow, dropping to a floor of waterlogged mud.

Grace Goddard (9)
Prestbury CE Primary School, Prestbury

Autumn

Autumn is like a bronze ship
that flies like a golden arrow
through the forest floor.
He is a scarlet paper plane,
that glides smoothly through the air
and over the trees.

He is like a dark flame
that scorches the trees
and burns through metal.
He is a golden feather,
parachuting in the bitter and crisp air.

He is a burning fire
spreading through the air.
He is a primrose that glows
through the air.
He is Autumn.

Alexander Moss (10)
Prestbury CE Primary School, Prestbury

Autumn

Autumn is like a thorn among a thicket
high above, now ready to descend, it falls into a mahogany heap.
She is a dying flame that once had a great life,
once so lively, once so bright, gently sinking into the night.
Autumn is like a soaring bird, perched on a tree,
golden, bronze and auburn, she's ready to take flight.
She is a silver arrow,
lying on the ground under the shimmering moonlight,
so sharp at the tip that it could pierce anything.
She is a feather sleeping on the ground,
so delicate and neat, all so soft in sleep.

Emily How (9)
Prestbury CE Primary School, Prestbury

Winter Treats

Icicles frozen, hard as rock,
Sometimes I wonder if the snow will stop.

Our cars are frozen on the path,
Whilst all the children laugh and laugh.

The trees glistening, sparkling bright,
There's a blanket of snow, paper white.

Children wrapped up from head to toe,
All ready for the snow.

The snowmen are waving, here and there,
The igloos keep the children from the wintry glare.

The children ready for their tasty treats,
Hot chocolate, cream and marshmallows in heaps.

Snow drops falling gently from the sky,
But it will soon be dry.

Freya Massie (9) & Molly Ellison
Prestbury CE Primary School, Prestbury

Snow Drops

The sound of snow drops
Patting against your shoulder
Pitter patter, pitter patter!

The blinding blizzard
Spraying against
Your face
Spray, spray spray!

The soft snow
Crunching like leaves
Under your feet
Crunch, crunch, crunch!

Sophia Lyon & Euan Davies
Prestbury CE Primary School, Prestbury

Autumn

Autumn is like a golden star,
tumbling in the golden breeze.

She is a scarlet flame,
falling from the sky onto the crumpled earth below.

She is a saffron sun,
illuminating the pale sky.

Autumn is like a golden feather,
slipping down from spider web to spider web,
then pointing to the ground.

She is a silky fabric, floating side to side,
surrounding the trees.

She is a crimson flame,
being dampened by the morning air.

Hattie Bennett (9)
Prestbury CE Primary School, Prestbury

Autumn

Autumn is like an opal coloured conker,
resting on the frost covered leaves.
She is a mahogany sunbeam,
coming from a scarlet fire in the damp and misty forest.
She is a piece of crumpled saffron coloured material,
shaped like an octagon, resting in the cold.
Autumn is like a rusty boat swinging from side to side,
as it gradually sinks to moist ground.
She is a bronze pumpkin, curling up more
as the weather turns bitter through the foggy season.
She is a russet flame,
tumbling and fluttering through the gloomy shadows of the sky,
reaching for a bed of leaves.

Nomi Fischer (9)
Prestbury CE Primary School, Prestbury

Winter Wonderland

Snowflakes falling from the sky,
Landing in my cottage pie.
Upon the window I can see
Snowflakes leaving friends behind me.
I look outside and what do I see?
Everyone playing, that's all I see.
I take one blink to see outside,
It's winter wonderland in front of my eyes.
A blanket of snow covers everything,
I make a pile and jump in.
I turn around and it's all gone,
What a disappointing time!
I really hope it comes again,
To visit me just one more time.

Molly Williams (10)
Prestbury CE Primary School, Prestbury

Autumn

Autumn is like a burning arrow,
firing down to the crumpled earth.
She is a sombre teardrop,
hanging willingly in the misty breeze,
Shuddering with every slight gust.
She is a saffron sunbeam,
shining on the mahogany floor,
illuminating the murky surroundings.
Autumn is like a piercing thorn,
ravaging its way through the uneven ground.
She is a hazel chestnut,
dropping through the autumn breeze.
She is a sleek parachute,
falling off a rocky cliff onto the damp earth.

Verity Partington (9)
Prestbury CE Primary School, Prestbury

Let It Snow

Let it snow
Snow falling all over
Building snowmen everywhere
Snowflakes falling down to the ground
Children playing everywhere

People sledging down the hills
Falling off, skidding off down the hill
When children are playing outside
They always say, 'Snowball fight!'

Getting wet, you need your wellies
Or snow boots and puffy outfits!
Get a hot chocolate, sit by the fire
Can't wait to play in the snow tomorrow.

Amelia Naden (9)
Prestbury CE Primary School, Prestbury

Autumn

Autumn is like a golden star,
swooping in the crystal clear air.
She is a saffron flame,
blazing in the burning fire.
She is a topaz petal,
blooming against the dying sunset with its amber light.

Autumn is like a clear teardrop,
dropping silently in the smoky surrounding.
She is a beaming thorn,
crashing onto the murky ground like an arrow.
She is a scarlet feather,
floating through the pure blue sky,
Gliding gracefully to the colourful bed.

Emily Green (9)
Prestbury CE Primary School, Prestbury

Snow

Snow feels like a star's dust
Soft and powdery,
As cold as a freezer.
It looks like feathers,
Falling freely.
It's a soft blanket
Covering the earth.

Kids wait in bed, expectantly,
As snow flies outside, peacefully
And patiently.
As it drifts slowly to Earth,
Slowly and silently.

Katie Pain & Mairi Florence
Prestbury CE Primary School, Prestbury

Autumn Days

Autumn is like a glimmering star,
lighting the midnight sky with a myriad of colours.
He is a sleek feather,
delicately fluttering to the dry, crumbling earth.
He is a jagged arrow,
swooping high in the crisp autumn breeze.
Autumn is like a crimson flame,
burning and illuminating the misty, sombre darkness.
He is a crumpled paper plane,
tumbling to the dripping grass below.
He is a smooth chestnut,
hiding amongst the beige twigs of the grand chestnut tree.

Noah Seaborn (9)
Prestbury CE Primary School, Prestbury

Autumn

Autumn is like a crimson petal,
dazzling in the gloomy sunset.
She is a shaking star,
fluttering gracefully in the drizzly air.
She is a hovering teardrop,
scuttling down to the waterlogged earth.
Autumn is like a parachuting thorn,
dangling from a slippery branch.
She is a paper plane,
tumbling down to a boggy floor.
She is a jagged chestnut,
collapsing through the misty shower.

Sophie Hiscott (9)
Prestbury CE Primary School, Prestbury

Autumn

Autumn is like a satin, topaz nut,
gracefully falling to the craggy, muddy ground below.
She is a tawny flame,
flowing down to the crisp, soft carpet of leaves.
He is a glassy, hazel chestnut,
swooping like a paper plane through the slippery branches.
Autumn is like a sleek, ochre nut,
tumbling down to a murky, bitter resting place.
She is a crinkled, sulphur petal,
showering down to the moist, smoky ground.
He is a rippled chrome arrow,
diving down to the dank, boggy ground.

Pippa Wyer (9)
Prestbury CE Primary School, Prestbury

Autumn

Autumn is like a saffron star,
gleaming in the dying sun.
He is a tawny arrow,
diving to the waterlogged ground.
He is an auburn thorn,
resting in a moist, craggy bush.
Autumn is like a mighty plane,
swooping through the misty breeze.
He is an ochre chestnut,
budding in its silky shell.
He is a copper sunbeam,
fading in the murky light.

Cameron McFarlane (9)
Prestbury CE Primary School, Prestbury

Autumn

Autumn is like a copper flame,
circling gracefully between the murky branches.
She is a saffron star,
twinkling in the midnight sky.
She is a crimson feather,
floating gracefully to the round Earth on the sleek, frosted air.
Autumn is like a hazel
tawny owl, flying to its baby fledglings.
She is an amber ring,
waiting beautifully to be worn by a soft, silky finger.
She is a chrome sun,
shining amongst the sombre.

Eleanor Bradley (9)
Prestbury CE Primary School, Prestbury

Autumn

Autumn is like a scarlet, crushed up berry,
dropping from the trees,
She is a colourful parachute,
Floating in the empty sky.
She is a tiny acorn,
hanging on to the leafless trees.
Autumn is like a giant mahogany chestnut,
dropping from the heavily laden branches.
She is a pretty petal,
tumbling through the myriad of colours.
She is a chilly teardrop,
diving to the damp earth.

Annalise Arkinstall (9)
Prestbury CE Primary School, Prestbury

Autumn

Autumn is like a sleek, mahogany chestnut,
basking in the bright, peaceful sunset.
He is a golden sunray,
shooting from the sombre sky.
He is a rusty plane,
gliding to the waterlogged ground.
Autumn is like a satin dress,
rippling in the bitter, autumn breeze.
He is a crumpled crisp packet,
tumbling through the gloomy forest.
He is a tawny fledgling,
shivering and lonely on the squidgy ground.

Kirsty Turpin (9)
Prestbury CE Primary School, Prestbury

Winter Wonderland

Snowflakes falling from the sky,
Landing on a mince pie.
A soft, snowy blanket covers the ground,
Falling down without a sound.
Snowballs flying through the air,
Snowmen built everywhere.
Children building a big wall,
Hoping that it won't fall.
Cars slipping on the track,
Whizzing round, it won't crack.
Marshmallows sizzling on the fire,
Children eating with desire.

Oliver Luckman & Harry Simpson (9)
Prestbury CE Primary School, Prestbury

Snowy Day

Snow, snow, let it fall
It doesn't bore children at all.
Make a snowman, make it talk
And make sure it can definitely walk!
Frozen icicles hanging off trees
Let it snow more
Please, please, please!

Marcus Jack Keenan, Alexander Dinnis
& Anna Palk (9)
Prestbury CE Primary School, Prestbury

The Snow Angel

Flying gracefully through the sky,
Dropping snow whilst passing by.
In the morning children awake,
To the snow on the freezing lake.
People trudging through the snow,
Gazing on the heavenly glow.
Looking up at the falling sky,
But nobody notices the angel go by.

Dulcie Whadcock (9) & Trudi Pennington (10)
Prestbury CE Primary School, Prestbury

Snowy Days

Snowy days, the trees are glistening
Children laughing and some whistling
While snow falls outside the house
Everyone is as quiet as a mouse.
Animals lurking in their holes
Foxes, rabbits, weasels and moles.
Icicles dripping from a rooftop
Everyone happy as they jump and hop.

Lucy Ridgeway & Roisin Tooher (9)
Prestbury CE Primary School, Prestbury

My Future

Looking to the future and what do I see?
How many children, one, two, three?
A husband and a dog and a really horrible job.
Looking to the future,
Thank goodness it's not me!

Sophie Parker (10)
Prospect Vale Primary School, Cheadle

What About Our World

Will the world be clean
when I grow up?

Will the planet gleam
whilst I'm still here?

Will the moon still be white?
Will the sunlight still be bright?

Will the trees still be green?
Will the plants be covered or seen?

When I grow and grow,
will rivers still flow?

Will sea be clean
and leaves be green?

Just imagine what it would be like,
if everyone carried on like this, every single night.

It's hurting animals, plants, everything.
It's even hurting the seabird's wing!

So stop it now,
For our health's sake.
A beautiful world
For us to make.

Jasmine Furness (8)
Prospect Vale Primary School, Cheadle

Emily

E xtraordinary Brownie
M ischievous monkey
I ce cream liker
L ollipop hater
Y oung panda supporter.

Emily Carson (7)
Prospect Vale Primary School, Cheadle

It Will Come

It is as strong as a lion's brawn,
But, unfortunately, it shatters easily,
It fades away like mist on the harbour,
As the damp, derelict, dingy boats leave port.
Memories of happiness gone
For another dying day.

Fighting will turn to it.
This of the biggest rivalries forgotten in the breeze.
Hatred, like fire, pushed out of reality.
A pendant of pride rises through the darkness,
To change hearts of solid stone.

Meanwhile, as change will come,
It obliterates the useless, damaging wars
Which create complete and utter unrest in the world.
But if it is destroyed, the Earth becomes as disrupted as a busy bee
When its nest has been destroyed.

Finally, in a world which has many imperfections,
It will break through like a bullet of harmony.
This is a hope for the future,
It requires our will to make sure that it happens.
It means peace . . . it will come.

Mohammed Ali (10)
Prospect Vale Primary School, Cheadle

Peace All Around Us

P eace is all around us
E verywhere we go
A mazingly diverse
C ountries all over
E ach and everyone to grow.

Hannah Evans (10)
Prospect Vale Primary School, Cheadle

Peace

Peace was all Jesus wanted,
When he came to this Earth.
But the Romans had other ideas
And arrested him and his peers.

Henry VIII then came along
And he had problems with peace.
He wanted to get married more than once
So he killed all catholic priests.

Next along came a dictator,
Adolf was his name.
He killed all the Jews in Europe,
World domination was his aim.

But Churchill saw him coming
And foiled his wicked plan.
He freed the Jews from all the camps
Because he was a peaceful man.

Now two thousand years later,
We still haven't learned from the past,
As wars are still going on all around us
And we wonder when there will be a peaceful flag on the mast.

Charlotte Brunt (11)
Prospect Vale Primary School, Cheadle

Snow

Snow is fun
Snow is cool
Snow is cold
Snow is exciting.

Sophie Clayton (7)
Prospect Vale Primary School, Cheadle

Think!

Think about the times you shared
And the times when no one cared.
Think about the people in Haiti,
They are sad and grumpy all day long
Because of the earthquake that stayed and did what's wrong.
They have had earthquakes here before
And they really don't want any more.

Haiti isn't the only place that's been tortured,
Jews, black Germans, Jehovah's Witnesses and gypsies were too.
Back in 1939 the Holocaust began,
The Nazis burst through the doors as the Jews ran.
People can take the time to remember what happened
Those 65 years ago
On the 17th January every year and don't do it alone
Get your friends and family to join in.

Think about our better future,
Children's futures and our world.
Think about, say something about,
Make it worldwide.
Think, think, think for once.

Ellen Corser (11)
Prospect Vale Primary School, Cheadle

Snow

Snow is exciting
Snow is fun
Snow is everywhere
Wherever you go
Snow is soft
Snow can crunch
Snow falls down from up above.

Maisie O'Neill (7)
Prospect Vale Primary School, Cheadle

Who Am I? I Am Aram

I am clever and I am funny.
I wonder about everything.
I hear birds twittering a song at my window.
I see squirrels jumping from tree to tree, trying to find an acorn.
I want a Nintendo DS!
I am clever and I am funny.

I pretend to play strict teachers.
I feel joyful and happy.
I touch real medium sized diamonds!
I worry about my brother, because he falls over a lot.
I cry when I visit my sister's grave.
I am clever and I am funny.

I understand that ghosts are real.
I say I believe in myself.
I dream about the whole world being made of
Cadbury's Flake chocolate.
I try hard in my school work.
I hope that Christmas will come earlier!
I am clever and I am funny.

Aram Shayan (9)
Prospect Vale Primary School, Cheadle

Our Future World

Tomorrow is the future, yesterday was the past, now is the present,
This poem is about the future! (tomorrow)

F ight for the future,
U nique it will be,
T ogether we can improve it,
U ntil it happens,
R emember to be caring to
E verybody and everything.

Lara Saxe (11)
Prospect Vale Primary School, Cheadle

Who Am I? I Am Rachel

I am sporty and adventurous.
I wonder who will win the X Factor.
I hear the shower in the morning.
I see the autumnal tree outside my house.
I want a pet dog.
I am sporty and adventurous.

I pretend I am a professional gymnast.
I feel happy because my teacher gives me a mini chocolate,
if I've produced good work.
I touch my hair.
I worry about speaking to an audience.
I cry if someone dies.
I am sporty and adventurous.

I understand that 5 x 5 = 25.
I believe in Santa.
I dream that one day I will have a dog of my own.
I try to watch less TV.
I hope to work with animals when I'm older.
I am sporty and adventurous.

Rachel Carson (10)
Prospect Vale Primary School, Cheadle

Look What's Happening To Our World

What's wrong with our world?
Why are we killing it?
Gas from exhaust fumes pollute the air.
It's getting harder to breathe.

Litter in the seas will strangle,
Cut or kill the sea creatures.
Stop Now!
We must save our world!

Molly Martin (8)
Prospect Vale Primary School, Cheadle

Who Am I? I Am Maleehah

I am happy and I am helpful.
I wonder what I am going to get for my birthday.
I can hear the rain hitting the roof tops.
I can see Mr Gray eating 20 Mars Bars!
I want the whole world covered in Cadbury's chocolate.
I am happy and I am helpful.

I pretend to win the X Factor and beat John and Edward.
I am feeling excited because it is Aaliejah's birthday party on Saturday.
I touch dazzling diamonds.
I worry if I haven't finished my homework.
I cry when somebody dies in my family.
I am happy and I am helpful.
I understand there are 365 days in a year.
I say don't listen to people who tell you to do wrong things.
I dream about flying Mars Bars.
I try to complete my homework on time.
I hope to become the world's best artist.
I am happy and I am helpful.

Maleehah Awan (9)
Prospect Vale Primary School, Cheadle

The Way The World Is

Will we survive or will we die?
Will the animals stay alive?
Carbon monoxide destroys the Earth,
Just imagine if we had no plants or animals.

Everyone damages the planet by dropping waste.
Toxic fumes kill sea creatures.
Why does this happen?

We should stop this *now!*

William Corser (8)
Prospect Vale Primary School, Cheadle

Who Am I? I Am James

I am curious and funny.
I wonder about animals and their species.
I hear my mum telling me to do my homework.
I see the TV screen blaring loudly,
I want a TV in my bedroom.
I am curious and funny.

I pretend to be like my cats.
I feel excited because it's nearly Christmas.
I touch the stars.
I worry about losing my teddy bears.
I cry when Manchester City lose.
I am curious and funny.

I understand $1 + 1 = 2$.
I say Jesus is real.
I dream about having a pet monkey.
I try to always do my best.
I hope to go to university.
I am curious and funny.

James Cottrell (10)
Prospect Vale Primary School, Cheadle

What About Our World?

Will our planet still be clean?
Or will our trees be cut down?
How will we breathe without oxygen?
Will our animals still be alive?
Will trees still be green and clean?
Will people care about our environment?
Why do people hurt out planet?
Will the birds still fly in the deep blue sky?
Will people still care about the Earth?

Sonam Rathour (9)
Prospect Vale Primary School, Cheadle

Who Am I? I Am Molly

I am hardworking and funny.
I wonder why wars started.
I hear wolves howling at the moon.
I see my brother crying over homework.
I want a Labrador puppy, called Buster.
I am hardworking and funny.

I pretend to be a worldwide dancer.
I feel excited because I am going on holiday.
I touch great white sharks.
I worry if I'll fall out with friends.
I cry when thinking of my brother.
I am hardworking and funny.

I understand my family love me.
I say angels and devils are true.
I dream about my big brother.
I try to keep my room tidy, but it always is a mess.
I hope to one day win £100,000.
I am hardworking and funny.

Molly O'Rourke (9)
Prospect Vale Primary School, Cheadle

Save Our World

Will there be an end to oil?
Will our world ever come to an end?

What if the rivers and oceans stopped getting polluted?
What if the environment got destroyed?
Will the trees get knocked down?

Will the cars and lorries stop polluting the air?
Will the ships stop polluting the oceans with oil?
Will the sun stop shining?

Samuel Jack Longman (9)
Prospect Vale Primary School, Cheadle

Who Am I? I Am Haider

I am brave and aggressive.
I wonder, will I be a footballer?
I hear John and Edward sing.
I see Mr Gray eating Mars bars.
I want an Xbox 360.
I am brave and aggressive.

I pretend I'm eating a Mars bar.
I feel excited because I can read the future.
I touch the Queen's crown.
I worry that Manchester United might beat Chelsea.
I cry when Manchester City lose.
I am brave and aggressive.

I understand that 0 + 0 is not 300.
I say that ghosts are real.
I dreamed that I got killed by a robber.
I try my best.
I hope I never die.
I am brave and aggressive.

Haider Sattar (9)
Prospect Vale Primary School, Cheadle

What About Our World

Why do people hurt the planet?
Will the trees still be green?
Will the sun be bright?
We have to look after the environment.
Just imagine if we didn't look after the world.
Will the trees still give us oxygen?
Plants and animals need our help.
We must work to save our planet!

Fizah Mahmood (9)
Prospect Vale Primary School, Cheadle

Who Am I? I Am Ben

I have blue eyes and blonde hair.
I wonder why kangaroos walk strangely.
I hear the planes coming over our school.
I see jack-o'-lanterns outside.
I want Manchester United to get relegated.
I have blue eyes and blonde hair.

I pretend to be playing a game with Manchester City.
I feel excited because it's nearly Christmas.
I touch fire.
I worry that I won't get any presents for Christmas.
I cry when Manchester City lose their games.
I have blue eyes and blonde hair.

I understand that monsters aren't real.
I say superstitions are real.
I dream about eating Mars Bars.
I try to score lots of goals at football.
I hope I will live forever.
I have blue eyes and blonde hair.

Ben Cottrell (10)
Prospect Vale Primary School, Cheadle

When I Grow Up

What will happen to our planet
If people are destroying it?
Will we survive or will we die?
Will the moon be white?
Will the sun be bright?
Will the plants still be green?
Will the trees still be seen?
Think about our future!

Holly Saxe (8)
Prospect Vale Primary School, Cheadle

Who Am I? I Am Megan Clayton

I am kind and I am helpful.
I wonder who are my friends sometimes.
I hear new music playing on my MP4 player.
I see a shadow in my bedroom.
I want a BMX for Christmas.
I am kind and I am helpful.

I pretend to be a pop star.
I feel happy because I am flying to America in nine days.
I touch the stars.
I worry about my baby brother at night.
I cry when my mum shouts at me.
I am kind and I am helpful.

I understand that I love my mum and dad.
I believe in Santa Claus.
I dream to be a pop star, just like Miley Cyrus and Cheryl Cole.
I try to clean my room.
I hope I will get a BMX for Christmas.
I am kind and I am helpful.

Megan Clayton (10)
Prospect Vale Primary School, Cheadle

Hope For Everything

Cross your fingers, close your eyes.
Hope for the better and tell no lies.
Hope for happiness, peace and love
Wishing on a star, high above.
No more wars, anger or sorrow,
Hoping all will change tomorrow.
Hope is something we should share.
Hope should be celebrated everywhere.

Olivia Cash (10)
Prospect Vale Primary School, Cheadle

Who Am I? I Am Daniel Dabell

I enjoy playing football and cooking.
I wonder what I'm getting for Christmas.
I hear my little sister singing.
I see birds in the sky.
I want a 60 inch television.
I enjoy playing football and cooking.

I pretend to drive a car.
I feel happy because it's the football team tryouts.
I touch lava because it is hot.
I worry about falling and breaking my arm or leg.
I cry when the bathroom door gets stuck.
I enjoy playing football and cooking.

I understand the sun is hot.
I say I believe in magic.
I dream about my holiday in Florida.
I try with my kick-ups.
I hope to be a billionaire!
I enjoy playing football and cooking.

Daniel Dabell (10)
Prospect Vale Primary School, Cheadle

Snowball

S chool has closed, I can have fun
N ow it's stopped snowing, I can play outside
O utside, I made a snowman today
W hen we left the snow melted
B ack yesterday, I made a snowman
A fter supper I made an igloo
L ast night it stopped snowing
L ook at my snowman!

Maria Chaudry-Hassan (7)
Prospect Vale Primary School, Cheadle

Who Am I? I Am Daniel King

I am friendly and happy.
I wonder why the Earth moves.
I hear people cheering for my basketball team to win.
I see Mr Gray eating a Mars Bar.
I want a dog.
I am friendly and happy.

I pretend I am on X Factor.
I feel excited because it's almost Christmas.
I touch food when I'm hungry.
I worry about my moon homework, because I think I haven't done it.
I cry when I fall out of bed and hit my head.
I am friendly and happy.

I understand that Mr Gray likes Mars Bars.
I say that one day humans will have gills.
I dream about having a pet gorilla.
I try to clean my room, but it always ends up a disaster.
I hope for world peace.
I am friendly and happy.

Daniel James King (10)
Prospect Vale Primary School, Cheadle

Hope For All

It would be good if there was no more hunger, war or suffering.
It is the world I would like to see.
Peace is everybody being happy and joyful.
No name calling, everyone is calm.
No harm being done to anyone.
So all be happy and we will live our lives in peace.
I love peace because everyone is happy and it is quiet.

Edward Wordingham (10)
Prospect Vale Primary School, Cheadle

Who Am I? I Am Nicola

I am happy and confident.
I wonder about all the different breeds of dogs.
I hear Santa tumbling down the chimney.
I see a camel climbing Mount Everest.
I want a pet gerbil, called Sid, who lives in a SpongeBob cage.
I am happy and confident.

I pretend to play the rock guitar.
I feel sad because I don't know what I want for Christmas.
I touched John and Edward backstage after the X Factor.
I worry about Manchester United losing the Premiership.
I cry when I am told off by my mum and dad.
I am happy and confident.

I understand that winter means Christmas is near.
I say that aliens are real and live in flying saucers.
I dream that I live in Candyworld with chocolate lakes.
I try to keep my cool when I lose my temper.
I hope chocolate soup will be made one day.

Nicola Diane Hall (10)
Prospect Vale Primary School, Cheadle

The Pollution In Our World

The pollution in our world,
The trees that are left.

It is not the past,
It is not the present,
It is the future.

The tree chopping,
The pollution of our plants and sea.

We should do something about it,
Something *today!*

Orla-Kate O'Neill (9)
Prospect Vale Primary School, Cheadle

Who Am I? I Am Zahra Choudhry

I am happy and I am helpful.
I wonder what I am getting for Christmas.
I can hear the birds singing through my ears.
I see dancing daisies.
I want kids to rule the world!
I am happy and I am helpful.

I pretend I am on the X Factor.
I feel jolly, like Father Christmas.
I touch the stars in the moonlit sky.
I worry if I am really injured.
I cry when somebody dies.
I am happy and I am helpful.

I understand that you should be fair.
I say don't give up, life gives you a second chance.
I try to do decimals.
I hope I can be on a TV show.
I am happy and I am helpful.

Zahra Choudhry (9)
Prospect Vale Primary School, Cheadle

Snowflakes

S nowflakes falling from the sky
N owhere in South Africa is snow
O bjects are turned into white, fluffy things
W ind is blowing through my mind
F lying through the wind in the freezing weather
L ooking at nature with beautiful butterflies
A frica is a very a hot place
K icking a football and having a lot of fun outside
E lves are making presents for Father Christmas to give
S inging Christmas carols to everybody.

Sanah Saghir (7)
Prospect Vale Primary School, Cheadle

Who Am I? I Am Aaliyah

I am happy and helpful.
I wonder what I am going to get for my birthday.
I can hear hoofbeats stamping along the sand.
I can see cute, black bears in Canada.
I want a small, cute puppy to adore.
I am happy and helpful.

I pretend to be rich, living in a mansion.
I feel excited because it's my birthday in a few days.
I touch the soft fur of a polar bear looking for the lost ice.
I worry that innocent animals will become extinct because of us.
I am happy and helpful.

I understand that my parents love me.
I say that you only get one life, so you should live it.
I dream about shooting the winning goal at a netball tournament.
I try not to talk in class.
I hope to get really good birthday presents.
I am happy and helpful.

Aaliyah Forbes (10)
Prospect Vale Primary School, Cheadle

Snowflakes

S now is great
N ow let's make a snowman
O ut we went and we made another one
W hen we left it, it melted.
F antastic snowman now
L oud, the wind blew off the head
A s the wind went we put it back together
K ind face and some of the body flew off as well
E ffort gone
S afe and sound.

Safah Choudhry (7)
Prospect Vale Primary School, Cheadle

Who Am I? I Am Hassan

I am funny and kind.
I wonder why my little brother cries when he loses.
I hear, on Saturday morning, my brother yawning.
I see my little brother secretly eating Mars Bars.
I want a good job in my future, so my family don't worry!
I am funny and kind.
I pretend to do somersaults on my mum's sofa.
I touched the glowing moon in the black sky.
I worry that Manchester United might lose to Liverpool.
I cry because my gran has passed away.
I am funny and kind.

I understand that the sun is a star.
I say there is only one God.
I dream about war dragons.
I try to do my impossible jigsaw in seven minutes.
I hope for my gran to come back to me.
I am funny and kind.

Hassan Rasul (9)
Prospect Vale Primary School, Cheadle

Do You Realise What We're Doing To Our Planet?

E veryone think, do you realise what we're doing to our planet?
A re we really being fair to the polar bears?
R emember plants, animals and the environment need our help before the ice melts!
T hink about pollution, litter on the ground. Do we not care about our world, or will the love be found?
H ow can we keep the sea blue? Will the grass stay green? Or will we just not care and the sun no longer gleam?

Now do you realise what we are doing?

Sarah Sweeney (8)
Prospect Vale Primary School, Cheadle

Hope Is With You

I am a tree,
I have seen winds and waves,
Hurricanes and floods,
Death and destruction.

I am a rock,
I have seen birds and beasts,
Hunted and killed,
Extinct and endangered.

I am Hope,
I have seen all this too,
But also times of justice,
People with honesty,
Acts of kindness,
Words of peace.
I am always with you.
Let's start again, together!

Kamran Chaudhry (10)
Prospect Vale Primary School, Cheadle

The Future

What will the future be?
Will it be with floating cars or buildings,
So high they touch the sky?
Or will the human race be extinct
Or maybe just the same?
Let's hope that World War 3 will not start!
So, I wonder, what will the future be?

I hope the future will be . . .
Everyone happy, caring and living a long and joyful life.
Maybe we might see aliens -
So, what does the future hold?

Kate Gibbons (11)
Prospect Vale Primary School, Cheadle

The Children

I see it on the news each day,
Another disaster far away,
Another war, here to stay.

Hurricanes, earthquakes, famine and war,
Drought, tsunami and many more.
It just isn't fair what these children endure.

These children should be having fun,
Not just sat in the blazing sun,
Some are even forced to carry a gun.

The world looks on and shares their pain,
Life for these children will never be the same,
Why it always happens to them, we can't explain.

I pray that a better future's in sight,
We must try to help them in their terrible plight.
Surely the way forward's for the world to *unite!*

Alex Robertson (10)
Prospect Vale Primary School, Cheadle

What About Our World?

Will trees give us oxygen or be cut down?
What will happen?
Who will be destroyed by this crime?
Will the world get covered in gas and doom us all?

Do you realise that Arctic animals might become extinct
Because of global warming from factories?

What about the sea creatures?
They could die because of our throwing waste into the seas!

Will the world end due to us polluting the air?

Please stop!

Ben Mills (8)
Prospect Vale Primary School, Cheadle

What About Our World

Will our trees still be green?
Will our planet still be alive?
Will there be trees to give us oxygen?
Will animals still be alive?
Why do we need so much power?

We need to
Save our country
And animal in
The world.

We need to
Save oxygen
To breathe.

We need to
Think about our
Planet.

Sonia Rathour (9)
Prospect Vale Primary School, Cheadle

Hope Of The World

Hope is fantastic,
Hope is what the people in Haiti need.
Hope is what they will need to live,
Hope is what will keep them fighting.
Hope is what will keep them strong,
Hope is what kept the people in Cockermouth
alive during the floods.
Hope is what kept everyone strong and faithful
during Britain's big freeze.
Hope will keep the people in Haiti faithful.
So I hope that you hope and pray
For the people in Haiti.

Thomas Pattinson (10)
Prospect Vale Primary School, Cheadle

Hope

I first appear as a wish,
A few moments later I grow into a want!
I quickly spread through the minds of humans,
As if I am a forest fire;
Burning straight into the heart of the lush forest.
I fill the empty hearts of humans,
Changing the way they think of me and you.

I am a breeze of happiness,
I am a wave of joy.

So what do you think I am?

I am hope!

You can live without food and water for days,
But you can't survive for ten minutes without hope!

You can't cope without hope!

Adam Pervez-Jan(11)
Prospect Vale Primary School, Cheadle

Our World

What's happening to our planet?
Is it in good hands?

Will our world be left in pieces?
Can we survive?

Will the sea be clear?
Will anybody be wiser?

Will there be sea creatures
Left free from man's destruction?
Our planet will last
If people help the environment!

Sam Crompton Whittle (8)
Prospect Vale Primary School, Cheadle

Change

We must make a change
Everyone must be kind.
A small portion of a wage
Can help someone blind.
Many of us may dismiss
The chance to help a disabled child
But we shouldn't hiss
Or let a child go wild.
Something as little as a pound
Could go a long way
To allowing a child who sleeps on the ground.
Have what they say
Help give someone a home
Or some water to drink.
Just don't let them roam
Or even go over the brink.

Rebecca Hall (11)
Prospect Vale Primary School, Cheadle

What About Our World?

Help the environment.
Save the world.
Will the food be healthy?

Will the sun be as bright?
Will we die or will we survive?

We need to stop throwing rubbish in the sea.
Will the trees still remain green?

Will our planet still be clean?
Will our animals live?
What does our future hold?

Kimya Arkian (8)
Prospect Vale Primary School, Cheadle

What About Our World

What will happen if
We don't look after our world?
Will we survive or will pollution
Take over the Earth?

Will the trees still be green
And give us oxygen?
Will the sea be bright and blue
Or will they be filled with oil and waste?

We should treat our planet
With respect and care for it.
If everyone helps
The world would be a better place.

So start now and don't stop
Caring for our planet!

Maddy Prescott (8)
Prospect Vale Primary School, Cheadle

Hope And Peace

We want hope not envy
For a door to open
Therefore a door to close
To see the light
To let go of the past
To carry on to a new life.

We hope for peace
As we see a man walking down the street
As that man gets older
A baby is born
To start a life
In a world of peace.

Zara Ashraf (11)
Prospect Vale Primary School, Cheadle

I Hope For A Day

I hope for a day when there's no more fighting,
Or guns blaring like thunder and lightning.
I hope for a day when there's plenty to eat,
Friends to hug and strangers to meet.
I hope for a day when all animals are free,
Whales in the ocean and fish in the sea.
I hope for a day when every illness has a cure,
For all people from coast to coast and shore to shore.
I hope for a day when children can be free,
To play like my friends and me.
I hope for a day when people don't die,
So people are always happy and never need to cry.
I hope for a day when crime is no more,
So we can leave open window, cat flap and door.
I hope for nothing more.

Mollie Hayes-Johnson (11)
Prospect Vale Primary School, Cheadle

What About Our World?

What will be left?
Will our food be fit to eat?
Will our toxic fumes
Clog up a crowded street?

Will the moon still be white?
Let's help the Earth
And not drive our cars every night.

Who will not become a victim
To theses crimes?
We can all do our part!
Even if we just put litter in the bin, not in the sea.

Please think and give our world respect!

Bradley Clegg (8)
Prospect Vale Primary School, Cheadle

Searching For Peace In Your Heart

People search for peace everywhere,
They shout, struggle and fight for peace.
Their need is one and only peace,
But what is peace?
What is it?

Peace means satisfaction in your heart,
The happiness you bear in your own life.
When you are happy and satisfied,
You will get peace in all aspects of life.

So searching for peace means being happy,
Bear that in mind.
When you get it you'll lead a very peaceful life.
You'll never need to search for peace again.
Never, ever again.

Sajeel Choudhry (10)
Prospect Vale Primary School, Cheadle

Peace

No war, no hate, no bullying.
No discrimination, no death, no fighting.
It's a better world we should wish for.
More cures, less diseases and better care
Shall be gained by hope.
People should think before they kill.
People should think before they declare war.
People should think before they speak
Because once the words have been spoken and heard,
It can never be taken back or forgotten.
Please think before you speak.

Robert Broughton-Smith (10)
Prospect Vale Primary School, Cheadle

What About Our World?

What will happen to our world?
Will it be safe when I grow up?
Will it still be clean?
What will happen to me?
Will I die or will I survive?

Will there be enough trees
To give us oxygen?
What will happen if to all the creatures
If they are poisoned in the sea
By fishing boats and liners?

Why do we need so many cars,
Vans and lorries?
Can't we just use buses?
We should all think!

Erin Naughton (8)
Prospect Vale Primary School, Cheadle

What About Our World?

What will happen to the animals?
Will the people care about our world?
Will people stop destroying our world?
Will the animals die?
Will we die or survive?
We should care for our world and our environment.
We should care for our planet.
Will the trees still be green?
We are the world.
Just imagine.
Will the birds still fly?

Saba Amjid (8)
Prospect Vale Primary School, Cheadle

What Will Our World Be

Will our plants be clean?
And where will they be seen?

Will our animals still grow?
And our rivers continue to flow?

When I am older, will the sea be litter free?

Just imagine . . .

We must fight this crime
Of pollution!

Rebecca Mulligan (9)
Prospect Vale Primary School, Cheadle

Snowman

S uddenly snow fell from the sky
N umbers of people went to play
O ut they went
W aves more came down
M ost was squashed into ice
A nd finally it went away
N ow we are back at school.

Jack Stelfox (7)
Prospect Vale Primary School, Cheadle

Kobe

K nows all about football
O nly hates his sister
B eing good at football
E ats lots of pizza.

Kobe Nelson (7)
Prospect Vale Primary School, Cheadle

A Better Future

Let's all start with a better future,
With tremendous teachers and tutors.
Always remember the people who have died,
Not to mention the ones in my mind.
All I want you to remember
Is to be a member of
The road to a better future!

Muazzam Naru (11)
Prospect Vale Primary School, Cheadle

Hope

H atred is spreading
O ptimists are extremely good
P eople are safely treading
E veryone should not feel sad.

Aliza Mian (10)
Prospect Vale Primary School, Cheadle

The Silent Classroom

Inside the silent classroom, nibs scratched paper.
Outside, Praise listened at the doorway for a cue to walk in.
The teacher sat and wrote tips on all their work.
While Praise stood, one hand on the door, to suddenly spring inside.

The children stood up to collect their work
and give the teacher their next piece.
Whilst Praise stood, watching and waiting to go in and say a word.
Silently the children sat and watched
and learned from an auto-computer.
While Praise sat writing all that was going on.

The children walked to get their new science books.
While Praise stood and suddenly rang a bell.
The teacher stopped and looked around and went to open the door.
She opened it and this is what she saw;
Praise stood up and gracefully walked through the door,
To shine on all the children and make them talk once more.

Eve-Marie Connolly (10)
Rose Hill Primary School, Marple

The Tree

In the dust-ridden, windy moors stood a humungous old oak tree,
His long, chunky arms swayed slowly side to side
in the gentle breeze.
His hard, slender skin crinkles in the fierce winds,
like he'd been in the shower for days.
His hair swooped and swished in the darkness of the night.
As his blood pounded through his body
like a twister inside of himself.
His fiercely big feet crumbled underneath the ground
As if it was an earthquake, but with a large amount of sound.
His whole body creaked and cracked as he awoke the next day.
Then his horrific feet crumbled and he crashed onto the ground.

Ella Dina Vanstone (10)
Rose Hill Primary School, Marple

Waterfall

The waterfall leapt off the cliffs
Somersaulting into the pool below.

The tall cliffs opened their eyes sleepily
When they were sprayed with freezing water.

The clouds watched everything
Swaying gently in the wind.

The rocks gathered around the pool,
Cheerfully enjoying the show.

Lara Garrett (10)
Rose Hill Primary School, Marple

The Classroom

The working brain of the calm classroom is busy at work
The hungry sharpener is quietly eating the petrified pencils
in the corner
The pointy pencils are slowly wasting away
While they are busy writing in the brightly coloured books
The chatty chalk talks with the bossy blackboard
as it squeaks and scratches
The snappy scissors eat away the paper
as they chomp, chomp, chomp at it.

Amy Smith (10)
Rose Hill Primary School, Marple

Will It Stay The Same? – Aztec Poem

The sun crunches as the wind gracefully leaps through the air,
Maize sings; trying to keep the rhythm with the shouting spears.
The moon laughs hard, whilst the temples hum to the chillies burning.
Black-eyed beans smile to the prickly cactus waving from across the field.
Floating gardens fly behind with joy and great proudness.
But will everything stay the same?

Sarah Tetlow (11)
Rose Hill Primary School, Marple

My Sister

My sister's a candyfloss machine.
She's always whizzing around.
Everyone thinks she's so sweet.
I wish she'd get eaten!

Harry Turner (10)
Rose Hill Primary School, Marple

The Tree

In the dark, dingy woods stood a dirty, hollow tree.
His mass of thick, pine hair blowing in the strong breeze.
His rough, bumpy skin, just like a dried apricot.
Its strong, twisted feet cling firmly to the dirty, crumbling ground.

His fast, rapid blood flowing through his chunky, healthy body.
His powerful, bent arms held strong and steady up high.
In the dark, dingy woods stood a dirty, hollow tree.

Jemma Cliff (10)
Rose Hill Primary School, Marple

McLaren F1 Supercar

My tummy is pumped to the peak with unleaded fuel,
The muscles in my arms are filled with endless power.
The spectacular super speeds I can reach are quick.
The bolted wheels are my wheel-spinning, rubber feet.
The crystal clear windscreen is my huge, staring eye.
The engine is the heart and organs I need to live.
My chassis frame is the skeleton of my F1 body.

Jack Rowbottom (10)
Rose Hill Primary School, Marple

Carol Singers – Haiku

Boys and girls in groups
Their mouths moving with a smile
Books in their cold hands.

Cameron Stone (11)
Rose Hill Primary School, Marple

Animal Riddle

Quickly I jump gracefully with my strong herd
As we jump an amazing 120 centimetres
I am as elegant as a snowflake drifting in the air
When you carefully look at me in the distance
You can see my lovely antlers on the top of my ginger-gold head
Soon I shall grow up to be as strong as my herd
I have outstanding brown hooves
My tail is so small and fluffy
I am precious

What am I?

Olivia Norris (8)
St Andrew the Apostle School, Halewood

Riddle

I am really crunchy
And you find me underground
I am juicy
And I might make your tooth fall out
What am I?

Caitlin Eyres (7)
St Andrew the Apostle School, Halewood

The Day I Met Space

The dark hill was cold and bare,
The night I met her standing there,
Wandering the sky so vast,
A shimmering, silvery shadow she cast.

A flood of starlight followed her,
Not so much as a bat did stir,
The sleeping moon began to glow,
The wispy wind made the trees blow.

I forced myself to ask her why,
'Why, Madam, do you explore the sky?'
'It's my job,' she sighed, 'to patrol space
And this galaxy safe to keep.'

In a dazzling flash of light
She flew away into the night.
I wished so much that I could fly
Across the moonlit, starry sky.

Emily Rafferty (10)
St Gregory's Catholic Primary School, Bollington

South Africa

I went to South Africa and I went in my truck,
I went to the elephants and then I said, 'Yuk!'
Then I went to the lions and they said, *'Roar!'*
Whatever you do, don't open that door.

We carried on across the savannah,
Then I listened to some Hannah Montana.
Then out of the window I saw a rhinoceros,
It was having a chat with a hippopotamus.

Ellie Collins
St Gregory's Catholic Primary School, Bollington

Space

We are surrounded by space,
On top of the Earth's atmosphere.

Space is full of amazing things,
Planets, stars and galaxies.

The moon is grey,
Covered in dust.

The red planet, Mars,
Is the colour of rust.

There are millions of stars
In which the sun takes part.

Only the astronauts of Apollo 8
Saw the Earth rise in 1968.

Michael Revell (9)
St Gregory's Catholic Primary School, Bollington

South Africa

S outh Africa is hot
O ut of this world
U p from the sky so high
T o bring them rain you need to try again
H ot, hot, hot!

A frica is full of animals
F ierce ones, crocodiles and lions
R oaring and fighting
I would love to see the animals
C ould you take me there?
A frica, Africa, Africa!

Anna Bishop (8)
St Gregory's Catholic Primary School, Bollington

Nelson Mandela

S outh Africa, where Nelson Mandela was born
O pen the doors of his prison
U nderstand his message
T ell the world his story
H ope that he gave to his fellow South Africans

A Long Walk To Freedom is his book
F reedom he didn't have for 27 years
R ights for his people
I nspiring man
C harges that were untrue
A mazing that he became President.

Ellie Richards (7)
St Gregory's Catholic Primary School, Bollington

Space

S pace, a place where you and I will never know
P lanets, that are placed near the sun so the sun can shine on them day after day
A stronauts, who whizz into space in their rockets to find new planets, up in the big, dark place
C ircuit, that all nine planets are on, near the sun is where they stay
E arth, where we live until the Earth dies away.

Izzy Hughes (10)
St Gregory's Catholic Primary School, Bollington

The Day I Met Sun

The day I met Sun I was on a trip to Mars.
She was passing by and I said, 'Hi.'
She smiled at me and stopped awhile
And passed on her way again.
On the way back I saw her sat down in a frown
Just like Mars itself.

Isabel Quigley (10)
St Gregory's Catholic Primary School, Bollington

Space

S tars glisten in the sky
P lanets, big and small orbit the sun
A liens move east to west
C omets crumble, descending to Earth
E arth is cold, Earth is hot it watches the moon go round.

Alex Needham (11)
St Gregory's Catholic Primary School, Bollington

Why Fairness?

One tired dove that thinks that fairness is love.
Two folded wings that think that fairness is hope.
Three magic feathers that think that fairness is care.
Four daisy rings that think fairness is faith.
Five moonlight songs that think fairness is forgiveness.
Six starlight bells that think that fairness is a glass of clean water.
Seven hidden treasures that think fairness is a bed without nets.
Eight silver chains that think fairness is a child of 4 or 5.
Nine secret trees that think fairness is a breeze.
Ten keys to keep, that think that fairness is a handle
And one little dove, fast asleep.

Jodie Rowlands
St Mary's Catholic Primary School, Crewe

I Dream Of A Dream – A Stream Of Peace

I dream a dream of a distant land,
Where birds sing, blossom blooms,
Flowers grow and trees sway to and fro.
War didn't create this, it was peace.
This land I see with children like me,
They have a warm, welcoming heart.
How come, I wonder, when I wake up
My dream ceases to exist?
My world is full of danger, my best friend dead,
The cold, dwelling thought rushes to my head.
Flying bullets everywhere, bombs exploding here and there.
I'm just a girl who has lost her way,
Trapped by war and getting weaker by the day.
With no food and nothing to drink,
How does she manage people? might think.
Dreading the days to come,
I stand tall and soldier on.
Many wounded, thousands dead,
This is no life for me.
This is no life for me.
I dream a dream of a distant land . . .

Jessica Prophett
St Mary's Catholic Primary School, Crewe

Peace

You should not fear
It is OK.
You have nothing to say,
The war is not here.
You don't need to pray,
Just live like you do,
But this time you will be safe.

Chloe Webster (11)
St Mary's Catholic Primary School, Crewe

Peace, Donate, Save

What am I doing, sitting down every day watching TV?
Why do I have 3-4 meals a day?
Why can I have as many drinks as I want?
Why is my money lying there in my pocket
Saying, 'Donate me, please?'
I hear them cry,
Fear,
Famine,
War and thirst
Thoughts like this make me burst.
Hate,
Jealousy,
Need and death,
Words of sadness are on my breath.
Women can't even have babies in peace.

First I will help,
Second my school will help,
Third, the whole world will help.

Blake Bratherton (9)
St Mary's Catholic Primary School, Crewe

Peace Poem

Peace is the soft beating of a child's heart
Peace is in the world, peace is in our hearts
Sometimes the world will not have peace in it
But it will always have peace around it
Peace is always with us, in the air and in our hearts
War is just pain and sorrow
I hope our peace will go on forever
So let us ask God for peace all the time.

This is my wish.

Tara Moir
St Mary's Catholic Primary School, Crewe

Peace

The sun shines on a beautiful day,
The village folk gather to pray.
The scent of victory gracefully flows,
The ray of peace happily glows.

Guns fire, bombs flash,
The remains of the cities lie in the ash.
The game of the soldiers is gone with the gore,
The Earth can receive peace once more.

The olive branches on the trees,
Hold the peaceful elegance of doves on the breeze.
The wars of the world no longer exist,
Their peace is kept amongst the mist.

Peace is the source of everlasting love,
Peace holds the branches, held happily above.
The sheep on the hillsides sit down for birth,
The peace is now locked safely into our beautiful Earth.

Lesley Anne Fox
St Mary's Catholic Primary School, Crewe

Why Are We

Why are we sitting here wasting away,
When fellow neighbours are led astray?
Fear, famine, war and thirst,
Things like these make me burst!
Why are we buying things we don't need,
When people are begging and we just have greed?
Death, hunger, people screaming, 'Why?'
Things like this will make me cry!
Things we can do are help and pray,
Then our friends around the world will be happy one day.

Trina Casanova (10)
St Mary's Catholic Primary School, Crewe

Elegant Dancer

Its intelligent waves shudder down into the misty open,
As it glides down to a lily so green,
Leaving only the slightest movement of a ripple.
Then, it scans the area, hoping to find nothing but peace.
Peace can be troubling and sometimes disobeying
But redeems itself in the mark of a dove.
With an enemy on its tail, in the shape of war,
It takes off with a pulse of amazing wisdom,
Dances on a soft cloud in a moonlit trance.
The Devil carries on, with a grin in its cold broken heart,
Sending bolts of rage to the bird of birds.
It dodges in alarm at the sight of this treason
with crazy determination,
Then it scatters off into the lush, golden meadows,
Knowing neither is beaten, but scared is the enemy,
For the dove is the sign of peace.

Isaac Orr (9)
St Mary's Catholic Primary School, Crewe

Peace Poem

Peace is always there,
Right in front of you.

It's right there, under your nose,
It's not that hard to find.

Once you've got it
There's no letting go.
Have it, take it,
Everyone needs it.

In the wars,
In our homes,
In our hearts.

Lauren Clarke
St Mary's Catholic Primary School, Crewe

Peace

Why am I so healthy?
Why am I so poorly and well again?
Why do I have so much from my family?
It's just not fair,
Yet I do nothing for my family!

Why was I so lucky at birth?
Why is my teacher so funny and prepared?
Why am I so happy and free?
It's not fair,
Yet I do nothing for my family!

What am I doing, sitting or lying in a nice, warm bath?
Why am I so rich and treated like I'm famous
When other people are dying, just like a bad game?
It's just not fair,
I am going to do something about it!

Summer Shannan (10)
St Mary's Catholic Primary School, Crewe

Peace

Why do I have everything I want for my birthday or Christmas,
Or even a special occasion?
Why do I learn to read and write?
Why is my school so perfect and I have good friends?
Why are all our teachers so prepared and good?
Why does the world have to fight every day and for months?
Why do people die from not eating or drinking?
Have you seen all the pictures of people that don't have anything
That we have right now?
How far is it to walk to get food for ourselves?
We can help people right now, by giving everything we can!

It is not fair!

Abby Lockett
St Mary's Catholic Primary School, Crewe

From A Distance . . .

From a distance
The world is a peaceful place,
With its mountains
Reaching into space.

From a distance
The world is a calm place,
With shimmering seas
Over my knees.

From a distance
The world is a full place,
With dull and joyful creatures.

Close up,
The world is an overloaded place, with war.
But we need to open a new door.

Leah Blake
St Mary's Catholic Primary School, Crewe

What's Fair?

Why have we got a school?
This world should be fair.
All the poor people are just sitting there,
This is not fair.
We should give money to all the poor people there.
Some people die,
Help them!
There's nothing there.
If the people die, you couldn't bear.
Food is good,
Hunger is bad.
Share now!
Be the good one!

Jordan Owen (9)
St Mary's Catholic Primary School, Crewe

Peace

When the battle rages and blood is spilled -
Peace.
When people fight and people die -
Peace.
When wars are lost or won -
Peace.
Whenever someone dies in vain -
Peace.
It is the alternative to war,
Saving lives, helps people survive.
It's when enemies become your friends.
Peace.

Caitlin Bayley
St Mary's Catholic Primary School, Crewe

Peace Poem

As the beautiful doves glide in the breeze
And the birds start to tweet in the old oak trees,
The guns and bombs will no longer exist,
And peace will come
Just like the mist.

The sun will shine on this beautiful day,
As the mice cuddle up in the golden hay.
The gentle lambs will start to give birth
And peace will forever be on our precious Earth.

Issy Pountain
St Mary's Catholic Primary School, Crewe

Peace Prayer

Peace is love
Represented by a dove

Peace is hope
That's why we have the Pope

Peace is brave
War is a slippery slope

Peace is in us
That's why we should trust!

Megan Brown (10)
St Mary's Catholic Primary School, Crewe

The Cat's Peaceful Dream

Why, I wonder, does mankind have to fight for victory through war?
Isn't it more victorious to be peaceful?
War causes suffering to people like you and me.
Would you like to play your DS at home,
Or be petrified of being bombed?
War is a nightmare to all nations.
This woeful world is full of war and crime.
I don't belong, not here,
I belong in heavenly cat world.

Aiqing Lu (11)
St Mary's Catholic Primary School, Crewe

We Need To Be Fair

Why am I special?
It is not fair.
We have lots of money,
We need to share.
Other people have nothing
And I am not bluffing.
I am embarrassed at death, need and want.
We should share,
Because we care.

William Ward
St Mary's Catholic Primary School, Crewe

Peace

Sometimes I sit all alone, thinking . . .
Why do I have a warm house?
Why do I have my own voice?
Why do I have a great family?
Why do I have all the resources I need at school?
Why do I have a funny teacher?
Why do I have medicine to make it better?

Think why I wrote this letter!

Gabby Williams
St Mary's Catholic Primary School, Crewe

Loving Peace

Why are children so poor abroad?
Why do people go to war?
My soul so weary and sore,
Mind bursting with cruel thoughts.

Thirsty for water and hungry for food,
Dirty clothes for children in sad moods.
Hate is poison to the kind at heart,
Open the gate to a peaceful life.

Daniel Cooper (9)
St Mary's Catholic Primary School, Crewe

Help Them

It's not fair, they have nothing.
Some nasty people think I'm bluffing.
Why do we do this?
It is so cruel,
When adults and children can't go to school.
We walk down the street with money in our hands.

Ellie Bolland
St Mary's Catholic Primary School, Crewe

Peace

You should not fear,
The war is not here.
Sad, hate, do not wait,
Run as fast as you can,
Don't stop, don't fear.
The war is never going to be here.

Emily Gresty (11)
St Mary's Catholic Primary School, Crewe

Peace Poem

Peace calls into your ears
So we don't want any wars
Peace is love
Just like the dove
Peace is giving
Peace is for living
Peace is from the Lord
So we need to stop wars.

Saffron Baldwin
St Mary's Catholic Primary School, Crewe

My Cat

Mouse catcher
Bird stalker
Fast runner
Tuna eater
Day sleeper
Night nutter
Paw licker
Treat chewer.

Emma Corby (11)
St Michael's Primary School, Widnes

Summer

Summer is bright,
The sun shines all around,
Children playing in the pool and on the beach,
Whilst parents, grans and grandads relax and get a tan.

School is out!
The children shout
Going on holiday to spicy Spain,
All the adults think the kids are pain.

Having six weeks off,
There is a lot to do,
Having fish and chips and curry for tea,
You're free to do what you want.

Having barbecues in the sun,
While eating your sausages in a bun,
Filling your tum,
Fooling around, not listening to your mum.

Callum Grimes (11)
St Michael's Primary School, Widnes

My Hamster

Food storer
Water gulper
Squeaky talker
Holder lover
Day sleeper
Night player
Fur tickler
Hamster fighter
Salad taker
Frantic digger.

Bethany Nolan (9)
St Michael's Primary School, Widnes

Me

M unching biscuits all day long.
O pen-hearted all the time
L oving and caring to everyone.
L ooking for chocolate in the fridge.
Y ells at her brother all the time.

F un to play with.
I am very playful.
L eaning over to all her friends.
L earning more every day.
I am fun to play with.
N ever naughty - well sometimes.
G ood as can be when I want sweets.
H appy all the time.
A lso very helpful.
M akes everyone laugh.

Molly Fillingham (10)
St Michael's Primary School, Widnes

Summer Sensation

Summer is fun, with ice cream and lollies,
Swings and slides all day long.
Children play in the paddling pools,
Having fun without any school.

Going on holiday to Majorca and Spain,
One-year-olds are a huge pain!
Mum and Dad always want to go on walks,
But all I want to do is sunbathe and talk.

For tea we have pizza and chips
And then we go home for a kip.
When we're asleep it's really hot,
Then Mum and Dad get in a huge strop.

Elliott Jenkins (11)
St Michael's Primary School, Widnes

Me

Calling her mum, for chores to do.
Always keeping my diary safe!
I am always looking for something to do.
Telling my mum my brother has bitten me.
Loving and caring, without a doubt.
I go rooting in the cupboard for chocolate and sweets.
Naughty, never!
Peeking in the door for chocolate and sweets.
All I do is laugh and laugh.
Raining, raining, all day long.
Eager to go hyper.
Running in and out everywhere.

Caitlin Parker (10)
St Michael's Primary School, Widnes

My Dog

Paw licker
Body sniffer
Food muncher
Biscuit cruncher
Bone lover
Bright clover
Lazy sleeper
Crying maker
Stupid waker
Tail waggler
Nose twitcher
Treat chewer.

Shannon Mercer (9)
St Michael's Primary School, Widnes

My Mum

Big-hugger
House-cleaner
Awesome-cooker
Night-sleeper
Biscuit-muncher
Teeth-cleaner
Day-walker
Meat-cruncher
Sleep-walker
Ball-kicker.

Nathan Jones (7)
St Michael's Primary School, Widnes

My Rabbit

Carrot lover
Box wrecker
Quiet squealer
Little sneaker
Wild drinker
Good jumper
Nose twitcher
Chocolate hater
Heart winner.

Curtis-Lee Campbell (11)
St Michael's Primary School, Widnes

My Sister, Aimee

Loud crier
Cool dancer
Animal lover
Ugly never
Good snorer
Quavers eater
Smelly pooer
My sister.

Louise Follon (9)
St Michael's Primary School, Widnes

My Mum

House tidier
Gigantic hugger
Brilliant cooker
Dish washer
Food buyer
Loud snorer
Biscuit muncher
Teeth cleaner.

Jack Clemson (7)
St Michael's Primary School, Widnes

My Cousin Louis

Unhlepful cleaner
Wotsit eater
Tea drinker
Loud snorer
Large hugger
Sleep walker.

Rhea Butterworth (8)
St Michael's Primary School, Widnes

My Brother

Loud screamer
Quavers eater
Weird talker
Jackson 5 soundmaker
Custard cream muncher
Carrot cruncher
Daniel misser.

Daniel Carroll (8)
St Michael's Primary School, Widnes

My Brother

Big snorer
Fun maker
Mad cleaner
Huge thinker
Silly singer
Milk drinker.

Frankie Carson (7)
St Michael's Primary School, Widnes

My Limerick

There was an old man called Bob
He went to see his friend Rob
He dropped his phone
And oh he did groan
A silly old man called Bob.

Dillon Barrow (8)
St Michael's Primary School, Widnes

My Spider Nan

Spider Nan, Spider Nan
Burns her bum on a frying pan
When I go to her house
She is eating a fat woodlouse
She is my Spider Nan.

Ellie Naughton (11)
St Michael's Primary School, Widnes

Human

Meat eater
Toilet seater
Plant chopper
Ground stomper
House liver
Cold shiverer
Water sipper
Pancake flipper
Film maker
Bread baker
Happy beamer
Sweet dreamer.

Luke Jamieson (9)
Sunnymede School, Birkdale

Snow

Snow!
Ghost-like,
Innocently falling down,
Beautiful, like a feather.
As gentle as can be.
Always floating down, without a sound.
Like pouring sugar very slowly.
Just like an angel.
Amazing snow fights.
So slowly,
Snow!

Nathan Chinn (9)
Sunnymede School, Birkdale

Cow

Grass chomper
Heavy sleeper
Lawn mower
Slow mover
Calf mother
Car stopper
Milk giver
Meat hater
Big eater
Leather maker
Moo talker.

Tosin Oyebola (10)
Sunnymede School, Birkdale

Hedgehog

Night creeper
Day sleeper
Slow walker
Prickly peeper
Cold keeper
Small weeper
Amazing hider
Spiky nipper
Freaky kisser
Fast eater
Horrible hugger.

Charles Carney (10)
Sunnymede School, Birkdale

Rabbit

Small hopper
Nose twitcher
Carrot eater
Vegetable muncher
Nature smiler
Grass creeper
Smiley licker
Tick flicker
Cabbage cruncher
Fluffy jumper.

Joshua Quinlan (9)
Sunnymede School, Birkdale

Parrot

Cheeky charmer
Rainbow flasher
Furious flapper
Chatter maker
Chippy chanter
Treasure seeker
Beach lover
Pirate liker
Loud squawker.

Isabella Knowler (9)
Sunnymede School, Birkdale

Dragon

Fire blower
Furious flapper
Night chaser
Tree scorcher
Meat eater
Tail swisher
Night creeper
New Year bringer
Day sleeper.

Skye-Bleu Trevalyan (9)
Sunnymede School, Birkdale

Monkey

Tree swinger
Coconut dropper
Banana peeler
Cheeky trickster
New Year bringer
Snide stealer
Risk taker
Beach boogier.

Katie Howard (9)
Sunnymede School, Birkdale

Hedgehog

Night creeper
Hand prickler
Worm eater
Bush sneaker
Rare sighter
Day hider
Winter sleeper
Summer waker.

Sam Harris (9)
Sunnymede School, Birkdale

Butterfly

Fast flyer
Nectar drinker
Cocoon breaker
Former caterpillar
Brilliant swayer
Spring enjoyer
High riser.

Emma Pitman (9)
Sunnymede School, Birkdale

Winter Weather

Snow gently twirls and dances
Along the long road to the ground,
Slowly painting the country white.
The snow appears to be moulding its own model,
Gradually getting bigger.

The icicles hang from rooftops,
Like fingers reaching out towards people below.
Ducks slip and slide across the frozen pond,
Motorways freeze over and cars go ice skating.

The snow falls faster and faster,
Quickly turning into a blizzard,
Fighting the people who dare to go outside
And Jack Frost spreads his icy fingers all over the world.

Emily Wallbank (11)
Winwick CE Primary School, Winwick

Eight Below

The temperature drops to minus 10 degrees,
The wind blows an icy breeze across the sky.
Roads are tucked in with a thick blanket of snow,
Until trucks come by, in the early morning, and take it away again.

The snow turns into large cotton buds,
Piles onto the ground, making the nation its own.
Robins bury their feet in the icy ground,
Shaking the snow out of their once cosy nest!

Icicles hang over windows, like giant animal claws,
Car drivers are Eskimos, trapped inside igloos.
Jack Frost visits every night
In search of a cold breeze to carry him home.

Eleanor Smith (11)
Winwick CE Primary School, Winwick

Winter Weather

The white snow falls like a soft blanket,
The bare trees sway lightly in the breeze,
The crunchy snow piles up, causing traffic jams.

Snowflakes fall gently,
The silent street is covered with cotton buds,
And the snow looks like tissue paper.

Blizzards dash around, sweeping up everything,
Ice and snow covers the cars and turns them completely white.

Snowballs melt quickly when you hold them,
And people put on their winter wellies,
Jack Frost peeps through your window!

Sandra Habeeb (11)
Winwick CE Primary School, Winwick

Winter Poem

Snow dances in the cold wind,
England becomes the North Pole.
Trees turn to white mushrooms,
Icicles are crying in the snow.
Roads become bowling alleys,
Cars turn into polar bears.
Small Minis turn into Land Rovers,
Golf balls change to snowballs.
House become white arrows,
Blizzards make white deserts in the countryside.
Children come back as snowmen.
Umbrellas change to frozen fountains.

Elliott Brooks (10)
Winwick CE Primary School, Winwick

Winter

Raging blizzards dash around wildly,
Blinding everything they see.
Ducks slip and slide on the frozen ice rink,
Cracks appear!
Jack Frost races around the world,
Delicately touching the earth with his icy fingertips.
Snowflakes are falling like clouds,
Swirling and twirling on the winter's wind.
Slushy snow sleeps silently.

Emily Noble (11)
Winwick CE Primary School, Winwick

Snow

Earth is wrapped tightly in a soft, white blanket
And families are cooped up in their homes.
Snow dances elegantly around me
And turns my coloured clothes white.

Jack Frost spreads his icy wrath,
Making it like a new ice age outside.
Ice hides, waiting for me to slip
And cars refuse to drive down icy roads.

Matthew Gardner (10)
Winwick CE Primary School, Winwick

Snow

Snow paints the countryside, cold and white,
Snowflakes dance to the ground like ballerinas.
Ponds are ice rinks, frozen hard,
Fish trapped under a ceiling of crystal clear, frozen water.
Ducks balance on the edge of the ice,
Cracks emerge!
Beware skaters!

Hannah Peake (11)
Winwick CE Primary School, Winwick

Winter

Snow floats around, like dust in the air,
Icicles are sharp as knives,
Like a ghost haunting the town,
Making people shiver,
Like sheep running loose.
Ice is a sheet of glass,
Like a mirror shimmering.

Brooke Lee (10)
Winwick CE Primary School, Winwick

Snow Poem

Jack Frost breathes over the world,
Black snow, like a Coke-flavoured Slush Puppy.
Naked trees wave at me in the cool blizzard,
Snow is ice cream that lasts for weeks.
The street becomes a bowling alley,
Cars race snails in the snow.

Matthew Hansley (11)
Winwick CE Primary School, Winwick

Snow

People trapped in their own home,
The snowmen population greater than the people.
Play has frozen at football stadiums,
Cars becoming icy glaciers.
Jack Frost nips at your nose.

Cody Griffiths (11)
Winwick CE Primary School, Winwick

My Poem

Frost on faces making noses run.
Snow lies on the ground like a soft, white blanket.
Ice is bananas on your feet!
Shining in the moonlight
Cars slip and slide on the bowling alley.

Jessica Bibby (11)
Winwick CE Primary School, Winwick

Young Writers Information

We hope you have enjoyed reading this book - and that you will continue to enjoy it in the coming years.

If you like reading and writing poetry drop us a line, or give us a call, and we'll send you a free information pack.

Alternatively if you would like to order further copies of this book or any of our other titles, then please give us a call or log onto our website at www.youngwriters.co.uk.

A platform for your poetry!

Young Writers Information
Remus House
Coltsfoot Drive
Peterborough
PE2 9JX
(01733) 890066

Get in touch!